THE CIA

THE CIA

BY
STEPHEN GOODE

Franklin Watts
New York / London / Toronto / Sydney
1982

Library of Congress Cataloging in Publication Data

Goode, Stephen.
THE CIA.

Bibliography: p.
Includes index.
Summary: Reviews the history of the
Central Intelligence Agency and its role
in world events since its creation
in 1947. Also discusses recent allegations
that it has misused its power and
engaged in illegal activities.
1. United States. Central Intelligence Agency—
Juvenile literature.
[1. United States. Central Intelligence Agency.
2. United States—Foreign relations—1945-
3. Spies] I. Title. II. Title: C.I.A.
JK468.I6G66   327.1′2′06073   81-21906
ISBN 0-531-04404-1   AACR2

CONTENTS

This Book Is Dedicated
To the Memory of My Cousin

Thomas Miller

1950–1981

CHAPTER ONE

THE CIA UNDER SIEGE

Is the CIA "a rogue elephant rampaging out of control?"

A question raised in 1975
by Senator Frank Church,
chairman of the Senate Select Committee
to Study Government Operations
with Respect to Intelligence Activities

The years 1974 and 1975 were difficult and trying times for the Central Intelligence Agency. Within a six-month period, the CIA was charged with allegations of wrongdoing and misuse of power—some reports said on a "massive" scale—that violated the laws of the United States as well as the laws of foreign nations where the Agency operated. The CIA had frequently been attacked in the past, but had always ignored the attacks and continued business as usual. The utmost secrecy was essential to intelligence work, CIA officials believed, and it would be dangerous for the Agency to become involved in public controversy.

In 1974 and 1975, however, the CIA could not avoid public controversy. The new allegations against the Agency quickly led to official investigations of CIA activities at home and abroad. These investigations, one by a presidential panel and two by congressional committees, revealed acts and deeds many Americans regarded as deplorable and wrong. Never before had any nation subjected its most prominent intelligence organization to such close scrutiny and criticism.

Many Americans, usually political moderates or liberals, praised the investigations and believed them long overdue.

They believed the CIA had exceeded its authority—and needed taming. Other, more conservative Americans, however, wondered if the investigations were a good idea. The CIA, they pointed out, was an important part of America's cold war confrontation with the Soviet Union and world communism. And any investigation that might weaken the CIA would also weaken the United States and play into the hands of its enemies.

The Allegations Against the CIA

On September 8, 1974, a confidential letter appeared in the *New York Times* and the *Washington Post*. The letter had been written by Representative Michael Harrington (Democrat, Massachusetts) to Representative Thomas Morgan (Democrat, Pennsylvania), the chairman of the House Foreign Affairs Committee. Harrington brought to Morgan's notice *secret* testimony by CIA Director William Colby which indicated that the CIA had played an important role in the internal affairs of Chile between 1970 and 1973.

The information was startling because two American presidents, Richard Nixon and Gerald Ford, as well as a former CIA director, Richard Helms, had denied any American involvement in the political life of Chile. Moreover, Harrington's letter raised questions about the morality of CIA actions in Chile—whatever they may have been—because the Chilean government had been overthrown in 1973 and replaced by a government that had abandoned Chile's long tradition of free, democratic elections. Had the CIA, critics asked, been involved in the destruction of democracy in Chile?

The furor and controversy raised by the Harrington letter was immediate and widespread. Senator Frank Church (Democrat, Idaho) declared that he was "incensed" by the revelations. Senator Edward Kennedy (Democrat, Massachusetts) said that the CIA operation in Chile "represents ... a flagrant violation of our alleged policy of nonintervention in Chilean affairs" and "an appalling lack of forthrightness with the Congress" about these matters.

Newspaper editorials likewise joined in the condemnation of the alleged CIA activities. The *Baltimore Sun* described the role played by the United States as one "steeped in hypocrisy and ineptitude." The *Charleston Gazette* of Charleston, West Virginia, declared that "what our government did in Chile was vile, vicious, contemptible, dishonorable—an action not apt to be forgotten either in South America or throughout the third world."

Further allegations against the CIA appeared in the *New York Times* on December 22, 1974, in an article by Seymour Hersh, a highly regarded investigative reporter. Hersh wrote that the CIA had conducted "a massive, illegal domestic intelligence operation during the Nixon Administration against the antiwar movement and other dissident groups." The entire operation, Hersh noted, was illegal because it violated the CIA's 1947 charter which forbade intelligence activity by the CIA within the borders of the United States.

In subsequent articles, *New York Times* reporters found a pattern of illegal domestic activities reaching back to the early 1950s. These activities included break-ins into the private homes and offices of American citizens, wiretappings, and the opening and reading of private mail. The articles also described the existence of a top-secret unit in the CIA that maintained files on thousands of Americans, including many prominent, well-known individuals.

The allegations of CIA activity at home raised an even greater amount of concern and apprehension throughout the nation than had the charges of the operation in Chile. The *St. Petersburg Times* said that it was "outraged" and that "it was long past time to bring the CIA under control, not only as to some of its offensive actions abroad, but also, now more than ever, as to its illegal assumption of secret police powers at home." The *Dallas Morning News* believed that the charges of domestic spying by the CIA should send "shudders of apprehension through all Americans who revere this country's constitutional freedoms."

A third set of allegations broke on February 28, 1975. Daniel Schorr, the Washington correspondent for CBS News, announced that former CIA director James Schlesinger, while head of the Agency, had uncovered evidence that the Agency was involved in assassination plots against at least three foreign leaders. The evidence had come to light, Schorr said, when Schlesinger asked CIA employees to report to him any questionable activities the Agency had committed in the past. As a result of this discovery, Schlesinger had ordered an end to any future involvement by the CIA in assassination plots or any similar activity.

Editorialists throughout the country once again condemned the CIA for its excesses. To many in the Agency it seemed as though America's intelligence community was under siege— and threatened with its very existence. The men and women who served the CIA and who believed their work to be patriotic and necessary to the survival of the United States now found their activities censured and denounced.

In addition to the allegations of involvement in Chile, wrongdoing at home, and assassination plots, other rumors also surfaced in the press during this period of controversy. The CIA, it was said, had experimented with LSD and other mind-altering drugs. It had manufactured and stored biological and chemical weapons of questionable international legality. And it had supported and abetted opium trafficking in Southeast Asia.

At the height of the controversy, Tom Braden, a prominent Washington political commentator, wrote an article on the CIA for the April 5, 1975, *Saturday Review*. Braden had been a division chief in the CIA during the 1950s and a close associate of the most famous of all CIA directors, Allen Dulles. But the revelations of the 1970s caused Braden to sour on the Agency and to become one of its chief critics.

"What's wrong with the CIA?" Braden asked in his article, and answered: power, arrogance, and secrecy. Power was the first element that had corrupted the Agency. "There was too much of it," Braden wrote, "and it was too easy to bring to bear—on the State Department, on other government agencies, on the patriotic businessmen of New York, and on the foundations whose directorships they occupied." As a result, the CIA's "power overwhelmed the Congress, the press, and therefore the people."

The arrogance of the CIA, Braden continued, caused its employees and officials to behave like a "power elite" which assumed that it could make the best choices for the nation without consultation with the Congress or the people. The Agency's penchant for secrecy made it highly insular and unresponsive to outside advice and recommendations.

The result, Braden concluded, was the creation of a "monstrosity" that no longer served the nation's intelligence needs—and which badly needed reform. Braden had no doubt that America needed the CIA as an intelligence-gathering organization. What it didn't need was an Agency corrupted by its own excesses and plagued by an exaggerated concept of its importance and power.

The Investigations

The allegations against the CIA came at a time when the American public and the Congress were demanding openness and forthrightness in government. The long, controversial war in Vietnam had aroused deep suspicions and doubts about decision making in high office. The Watergate Affair had only recently resulted in the resignation and the imprisonment of many of the president's associates for abuse of authority and other crimes. In the post-Vietnam War and post-Watergate atmosphere of Washington, the charges against the CIA could not be ignored or swept under the table.

On January 5, 1975, less than two weeks after the story of CIA domestic activity had broken, President Gerald Ford named a "blue ribbon" panel to "determine whether the CIA had exceeded its statutory authority" and also to look into "whether existing safeguards are adequate to preclude agency activities that might go beyond its authority." The panel was also charged with the responsibility to make recommendations that might improve the CIA.

Ford chose Vice-President Nelson Rockefeller to head the panel, which was known as the Rockefeller Commission. Rockefeller had broad experience in government and was a member of the president's Foreign Intelligence Advisory Board, a committee of civilians that met regularly to review the nation's intelligence network and its activities. The "blue ribbon" panel included seven other prominent Americans, among them Lane Kirkland, secretary-treasurer of the AFL-

[6]

CIO, Lyman Lemnitzer, the chairman of the Joint Chiefs of Staff during the Kennedy administration, and Ronald Reagan, the former governor of California, who would later become president.

The Senate did not lag far behind. On January 27, 1975, it voted 82 to 4 to establish a bipartisan select committee to investigate the allegations of illegal CIA domestic activity and other abuses of power by the Agency. The committee was charged to determine "the extent, if any, to which illegal, improper or unethical activities were engaged in by any agency or by any persons, acting either individually or in combination with others, in carrying out any intelligence or surveillance activities by or on behalf of any agency of the federal government."

Senator Frank Church was appointed chairman of the committee. The Vice-Chairman was John Tower, a Republican from Texas. They were to be assisted by nine other senators, including Walter Mondale of Minnesota and Gary Hart of Colorado for the Democrats and Barry Goldwater of Arizona and Howard Baker of Tennessee for the Republicans. The committee reflected a broad range of views, from conservatives Goldwater and Tower to liberals Mondale and Church.

On February 19, the House of Representatives followed suit. By a vote of 286 to 120, it created a select committee to look into all charges of "illegal or improper" intelligence activities by government agencies. Representative Lucien Nedzi (Democrat, Michigan) was named chairman of the committee, to which seven Democrats and three Republicans were appointed.

During the following months, the Rockefeller Commission concentrated its investigation on the CIA activities within the United States. The Senate Select Committee looked primarily at the alleged abuses abroad. Both groups would receive praise from the press and other media for dispassionate, thorough studies at the conclusion of their work. With the House Select Committee, however, it was different. Plagued from the beginning by disputes and quarrels among its members, the House committee gained more notoriety for its inability to conduct an orderly investigation than praise for the quality of its research and the accuracy of its findings.

The National Security Debate
At the root of the controversy over the CIA lies the question of national security. Defenders of the Agency point out that the CIA plays an essential role in modern American life. It provides the president with up-to-date information on the goals and intentions of the Soviet Union and other foreign nations. Without this information, the President would be hard-pressed to make the best possible decisions on foreign policy and on the best course of action the country should take in times of crisis.

Moreover, the defenders continue, the CIA is the chief means at America's disposal to confront world communism. The CIA's Soviet counterpart, the KGB, is the largest intelligence organization in the world. It spends large sums of money and is not bound by moral or legal considerations. Its agents are at work in almost every nation in the world, including the United States. Without the CIA, the United States would have no way to challenge and overcome the KGB on its own terms.

It is not surprising, this argument runs, that the work of the CIA should often appear devious, underhanded, illegal, or immoral. Such is the nature of the modern world and of the confrontation between the Soviet Union and the United States. "You have to make up your mind," Senator John Stennis (Democrat, Mississippi) said at a hearing in 1971, "that you are going to have an intelligence agency and protect it as such, and shut your eyes some and take what is coming."

The problem in the 1970s was that few people seemed to be taking Stennis' advice. For defenders of the Agency this amounted to putting a loaded gun in the hands of America's enemies. "I am indignant," former CIA Director Richard Helms said in January, 1975, "at the irresponsible attacks made upon the true ends of the intelligence function." Helms believed the CIA was being unjustly—and dangerously—pilloried at a time when Soviet power was increasing throughout the world.

William Colby, the man who followed Helms as CIA director, shared Helms' concern about intelligence. One month after Helms' statement, Colby warned that "exaggerated" charges of illegal activities by the Agency "had placed American intelligence in danger." The almost hysterical excitement," Colby said, "that surrounds any news story mentioning the CIA, or referring even to a perfectly legitimate activity of CIA, has raised the question whether secret intelligence operations can be conducted by the United States."

The specific worries Colby had about the future of American intelligence were two. First, he believed that foreign intelligence organizations that had collaborated with American intelligence in the past would now refuse to work with the CIA because the CIA was under public scrutiny and investigation. This scrutiny and investigation, foreign intelligence agents maintained, would threaten the secrecy of their own organizations.

Second, Colby spoke of a malaise that was affecting CIA agents who believed their patriotism was being called into question. How could these men and women carry out their work if they found their activities questioned at every step? Moreover, CIA agents in the field now had an additional problem to worry about. Public scrutiny of their activities might make their names known to the enemy, and leave them open to physical attack or even assassination.

The defenders of the Agency ardently support the CIA as essential to the American way of life. But there is another side to the question. This other side was noted in a 1969 speech by President Richard Nixon. "This organization," Nixon said, referring to the CIA, "has a mission, that, by necessity, runs counter to some of the very deeply held traditions in this country and feelings, high idealistic feelings, about what a free society ought to be."

What were these "high idealistic feelings" that ran counter to the Central Intelligence Agency and its work? Nixon did not mention them in his speech, but the traditions he alluded to were clear. First was the tradition of America as an "open" society, where press and public could criticize government activities without fear of reprisal. Second was the belief that America was somehow "different" from other nations because it did not stoop to the tactics and methods employed by totalitarian governments. The revelations about the CIA seemed to show that the Agency had violated both of these traditions.

For the critics of the CIA in the 1970s, the violations of American traditions were significant and grave. The CIA, they charged, had adopted the tactics of the enemy and abandoned what was best—and unique—in American history. If this was the price that had to be paid for a strong and effective CIA, they concluded, then the price was too high. It was better to have a weaker intelligence organization than one that ran roughshod over the rights of citizens and turned the United States into a police state.

The CIA controversy, therefore, resolved itself into two opposing camps. On the one side stood those whose primary concern was the security and strength of the United States; on the other were those who emphasized individual rights and freedoms, even during times of crisis. Somewhere between the positions stood most of the American people, most of Congress, and most of the members of the presidential panel and the congressional select committees.

For these people of the middle position, the question was how to maintain national security and at the same time have an efficient, yet decent and honorable Central Intelligence Agency. If the CIA had committed excesses and exceeded its authority, then it should be brought into line—cautiously and carefully, because an Agency sapped of all its power would be as dangerous to the well-being of the country as one that had too much power.

President Ford voiced the opinions of the many moderates on April 7, 1975, when he asked CIA critics in Congress and elsewhere not to cripple "a vital national institution." America, Ford said, "will not give in to self-doubt nor paralysis of will power ... Americans will not dismantle the defense of the United States. And we certainly will not adopt such a naive vision of this world in which we live that we dismantle our essential intelligence-gathering agencies."

[10]

The Critics and their Criticisms

During the 1970s, criticism of the CIA concentrated in three general areas. First was the question of CIA authority and the extent of its power. Second was criticism of methods and tactics it employed. Third was the problem of objectives: what ends or goals had the Agency been established to achieve, and were these goals compatible with the best interests of the United States?

The question of CIA authority was complex. To whom did the Agency owe allegiance and to whom was it accountable? To the president, whom it advised on foreign intelligence? To the Congress, which had voted it into existence and provided its annual budget? Or was the CIA, owing to the nature of intelligence work and the importance of secrecy, a special preserve within the federal government where laws and regulations that applied to other agencies did not apply?

One critic who believed that the question of authority was central to the CIA controversy was Henry Steele Commager, a noted American historian. Commager wrote about the Agency in a 1976 *New York Review of Books* article entitled "'Intelligence': The Constitution Betrayed." In the article, Commager took the position that the CIA over the years had amassed a great deal of power to which it was not constitutionally entitled and for which it was not held accountable.

The Congress, Commager maintained, had the power to limit the CIA, because it controlled—at least according to the Constitution—the CIA's budget. But the Congress had proved too timid to exercise its authority and it had been left to the liberal press—newspapers and magazines like the *Washington Post,* the *New York Times, New York Review of Books,* and *The Nation*—to exercise vigilance over CIA activities.

The failure of Congress to exercise its authority over the CIA, Commager implied, had given the CIA license to exceed legal and moral restrictions that otherwise might have been placed upon it. Now was the time for the House and Senate to stand up and make the CIA accountable for its actions, just as Congress had made President Nixon and his associates accountable for their crimes in the Watergate Affair.

[11]

In their attacks on the methods used by the CIA, the critics pointed to a whole range of covert or secret operations employed by the Agency. These included assassination plots against foreign leaders and CIA attempts to destabilize or undermine foreign governments economically or politically. Any method used by the Agency that did not contribute to the collection of intelligence, the critics condemned. They believed that CIA activity abroad should be limited to the gathering of information for use in reports to the President.

The critics also attacked the methods the CIA had used in its domestic operations: the wiretappings, buggings, break-ins, and surveillance of mail. The methods used at home and abroad, they maintained, reflected the character of the United States and showed the world what America stood for. If these methods did not differ from those employed by the enemy, then there was little that could distinguish the United States from the Soviet Union or any other totalitarian government.

Finally, the critics challenged the CIA to define its objectives. Did the Agency make foreign policy on its own, without reference to the policies established by the State Department or the Senate? Was it primarily guided by a negative impulse to see communism eradicated everywhere in the world, or did it have positive goals, such as support for the spread and improvement of democracy?

The questions were important, because one thing that troubled the critics was what they believed was the tendency of the CIA to act on its own—and then pull the nation after it. Had the Agency, for instance, worked to destroy the government in Chile and then sat back as the rest of America had to accept the destruction of that government as an accomplished fact? What was needed, the critics argued, was a means to make the objectives of the CIA reflect more closely the objectives and goals of the American people and the American government as a whole, rather than the interests and concerns of a small group of men who dominated the intelligence community.

Among the more extreme criticisms of the CIA, two books stand out. The first is *The CIA and the Cult of Intelligence* by Victor Marchetti and John D. Marks, published in 1974. The second is Philip Agee's *Inside the Company: CIA Diary,* which followed in 1975. Both books have had widespread impact and played major parts in the CIA controversy of the 1970s.

Victor Marchetti was a CIA military analyst and Russian expert who rose rapidly in CIA ranks to serve in the office of the CIA director between 1966 and 1969. Once an ardent supporter of the Agency and its activities, he grew to distrust the CIA and came to the conclusion that it did more harm than good. He resigned his post in 1969 and turned his attention to writing. His coauthor, John Marks, worked in the State Department's Bureau of Intelligence and Research between 1968 and 1969, before he too left intelligence work.

Their book was one long indictment of the CIA.* The book opened with a warning. "There exists in our nation today," the authors wrote, "a powerful and dangerous secret cult—the cult of intelligence." The purpose of the cult of intelligence, they continued, "is to further the foreign policies of the U.S. government by covert and usually illegal means, while at the same time containing the spread of its avowed enemy, communism."

The cult of intelligence, of which the CIA "is both the center and the primary instrument," "thrives on secrecy and deception," the authors continued.

> *It encourages professional amorality—the belief that righteous goals can be achieved through the use of unprincipled and normally unacceptable means. The cult is intent upon conducting the foreign affairs of the U.S. government without the awareness or participation of the people. It recognizes no role for a questioning legislature or an investigative press. Its adherents believe that only they have the right and the obligation to decide what is necessary to satisfy the national needs.*

*All former CIA employees are required to submit any writing they do on the Agency to CIA headquarters for approval. Marchetti and Marks complied with this requirement and, as a result, their book was heavily censored by the CIA. The authors gained the right to publish some of the censored material through a court decision, but many passages remained deleted when the book when to press.

Marchetti and Marks agreed that "there can be no doubt that the gathering of intelligence is a necessary function of modern government." What they found intolerable about the CIA and the cult of intelligence was its presence throughout the world and its involvement in countless numbers of questionable operations. The CIA, they pointed out, "engages in espionage and counterespionage, in propaganda and disinformation (the deliberate circulation of false information), in psychological warfare and paramilitary activities." Moreover,

> It penetrates and manipulates private institutions, and creates its own organizations (called "proprietaries") when necessary. It recruits agents and mercenaries; it bribes and blackmails foreign officials to carry out its most unsavory tasks. It does whatever is required to achieve its goals, without any consideration of the ethics involved or the moral consequences of its actions.

The authors dismissed the notion that the CIA maintains secrecy around its activities in the interest of national security. "The fact is," they concluded, "that in this country, secrecy and deception in intelligence operations are as much to keep the Congress and the public from learning what their government is doing as it is to shield these activities from the opposition."

Secrecy and deception, too, disguise CIA mistakes and give the Agency the opportunity to "avoid accountability" and "maintain freedom of action." Marchetti and Marks want a CIA that has abandoned all activities except the gathering of pure intelligence. And they want an Agency open to public view and scrutiny. Only in an open Agency can the cult of intelligence be brought to an end and the proper activities of an intelligence organization be restored.

Philip Agee, on the other hand, would like to see the CIA destroyed. Like Marchetti, Agee is a former CIA employee who worked as an agent in Ecuador, Uruguay, and Mexico between 1960 and 1968. And like Marchetti, Agee joined the Agency with a firm belief in the importance of its work and gradually grew disenchanted and disillusioned.

Agee, however, stands far to the political left of Marchetti. A socialist, he defines the CIA as "the secret police of

American capitalism." The Agency, he claims, works "night and day" to plug up "leaks in the political dam ... so that shareholders in U.S. companies" which operate in poor countries "can continue enjoying" the profits they make from their exploitation of the third world.

Agee's first book on the Agency, *Inside the Company: CIA Diary,** is a detailed look at his twelve years in the CIA from the time of his recruitment and initial training through his resignation in 1969. The story he tells is one of deceit, hypocrisy, and corruption, where CIA agents serve American interests and the interests of the ruling elites in Latin America.

For Agee, the CIA is an evil force that prolongs the misery of the poor and powerless. It has established a vast and complex web of political and economic influence in the countries of Latin America and elsewhere, a web that includes labor unions, political parties, prominent leaders, and many other aspects of the societies where the CIA is at work. Presidents, generals, and others have been in the pay of the Agency. In addition, the CIA has helped to train repressive police forces that regularly violate human rights and help maintain authoritarian governments in power.

Agee claims that the CIA revelations of the 1970s showed that the Agency's immorality abroad has spread to the United States. "For those who were unaware of the U.S. government's secret tools of foreign policy," he writes, "perhaps this diary will help answer some of the questions on American domestic political motivations and practices that have arisen since the first Watergate arrests."

"In the CIA," he continues, "we justified our penetration, disruption and sabotage of the left in Latin America—around the world for that matter—because we felt morality changed on crossing national frontiers." But now, he continues, it is obvious that the lack of morality the CIA practiced abroad was also practiced at home—with the same lack of concern for individual rights and democratic traditions.

---

*CIA insiders refer to the Agency as "the company." Unlike Marchetti, Agee did not submit the manuscript of his book for approval by CIA headquarters.

Agee's hatred of the CIA knows no bounds. He now lives abroad, in West Germany, and his passport has been revoked by the U.S. State Department in an action upheld by the U.S. Supreme Court in the summer of 1981. In his books and publications, he regularly reveals the names of CIA agents working in foreign lands, an act that "blows their cover," ends their efforts to maintain secrecy, and puts their lives in danger. His acknowledged aim is to disrupt the activities of the Agency, wherever he finds CIA agents at work.

This book will examine the controversy surrounding the CIA. In the next chapter, we shall look at the nature of intelligence work and at the origins of the Central Intelligence Agency. Subsequent chapters will trace the development, and rapid expansion, of that Agency from its small beginnings to the large and far-flung organization that exists today. The final chapters will return to the question of CIA wrongdoing in the 1970s and discuss the merits of the charges made against the Agency and the results of the official investigations into CIA behavior.

Throughout the book, one remarkable fact about the CIA stands out: the story of the Agency during its thirty-five years of existence is the story of the deepest concerns and fears of the United States. Founded at a time when the cold war was at its coldest, the CIA was part of America's system of defense against communist expansion. No one questioned the need for a central intelligence organization; its existence was taken for granted, like the standing army and the large defense budgets.

During the 1960s, however, when American institutions were called into question by the Civil Rights Movement, the antiwar movement, and the New Left, the CIA too began to experience its first widespread public attacks. These attacks grew in virulence and significance through the 1970s, when they culminated in the investigations mentioned earlier in this chapter. But the CIA was not the only part of the government to undergo challenge and reform in this period: similar upheavals also struck the presidency, the Congress, and the military.

After 1975, as political calm returned to the nation, a similar calm returned to the CIA. By 1981, when this book was written, the Agency seemed well on the road of recovery from the controversies of the 1970s. Renewed cold war fears about the power of the Soviet Union once again convinced the American public of the need for a strong intelligence organization. The charges that had been made against the CIA only six years earlier seemed to be forgotten. This book will look at the early years of the Agency, at its fall from grace, and then at its return to favor and prestige.

CHAPTER TWO

THE CIA AND THE NATURE OF INTELLIGENCE

"Policy must be based on the best estimate of the facts which can be put together. That estimate in turn should be given by some agency which has no axes to grind and which itself is not wedded to any particular policy."

CIA Director Allen Dulles

Intelligence has been called the world's second oldest profession. It has also been looked upon as a romantic calling, pursued by men and women of extraordinary physical ability and courage who crave excitement and challenge—the type of secret agent described in the popular James Bond novels and other spy thrillers. But it is probably safe to say that most people have little knowledge of the nature of intelligence or of intelligence work, especially in our time when advanced technology has made the world of intelligence complex and highly sophisticated.

The Nature of Intelligence

Webster's New Collegiate Dictionary defines "intelligence" as "information; news; advice" and as "the obtaining or dispensing of information, particularly secret information." Professor Harry Howe Ransom, the foremost American academic expert on intelligence, agrees with this definition, but would add that it does not go far enough.

True intelligence, Ransom maintains, is not merely information; it is "evaluated" and "processed" information "about the power and intentions of foreign nations or other

[20]

external phenomena of significance in decision-making councils." Without evaluation and processing, he adds, intelligence would not be worth much to the men and women who must decide on national policy.

Ransom categorizes intelligence into what he regards as three "useful" divisions: "strategic or national intelligence," "tactical or combat intelligence," and "counterintelligence." The responsibilities of strategic intelligence, he points out, are broad and important. In time of peace, strategic intelligence must provide long-range predictions of political, economic, and social trends throughout the world. It must be prepared to warn decision makers about imminent political and military actions that might affect the interests of the United States.

Ransom claims that any organization concerned with strategic intelligence will, by necessity, be an ever-growing and expanding entity. The reasons for this lie in the nature of strategic intelligence. Because the needs of strategic intelligence are so broad and all-encompassing, no realistic limits can be placed on organizations like the CIA that are involved in the acquisition of such intelligence. No one can say when enough information has been collected on a given subject; there is always the uncomfortable suspicion that a few more facts might bring a partially understood situation into focus.

Ransom's second type of intelligence—tactical or combat intelligence—concerns information that military commanders need in field operations during war. Only rarely is an agency like the CIA involved in the collection of intelligence of this type, which is customarily left to the military intelligence units in the Army, Navy, and Air Force.

The third category of intelligence, counterintelligence, however, plays an important part in the work of the CIA. Counterintelligence is sometimes referred to as "negative intelligence." It seeks to prevent enemy agents from obtaining secret information about the United States and conducts programs that help to protect and conceal American military installations and other top-secret projects from espionage or sabotage. Counterintelligence employs various methods of concealment, camouflage, codes and ciphers, and deception in order to trick and outwit the enemy.

Counterintelligence is also responsible for the uncovering and identification of individuals or groups that may be planning to carry out espionage or sabotage. In recent years, with the rapid increase in terrorist activity throughout the world, this responsibility has taken on a new importance. Antiterrorist units within the CIA have been improved and strengthened, and terrorism has become a "number one" priority at the Agency.

In addition to the three categories mentioned above, there are two other general terms associated with intelligence that should be defined: "espionage" and "counterespionage." Espionage is the secret or clandestine collection of intelligence through illegal methods. Most intelligence is gathered from "open" sources, that is, from monitored radio programs or published materials that are collected and analyzed by specialists. Espionage, on the other hand, is the work of the spy or secret agent, who risks arrest—and death—for his work.

Counterespionage is the clandestine and secret side of counterintelligence. According to a definition coined in a secret report during World War II, counterespionage not only attempts to protect the intelligence interests of the government it serves, but also seeks "the control and manipulation of the intelligence operations of other nations" in the hope of discovering "the plans and intentions" of enemy espionage units.

One method employed by counterespionage is the use of the "double agent." A double agent pretends to serve loyally the intelligence organization to which he belongs while actually working for the enemy. He or she serves two purposes. First, a double agent is a source of valuable information about the methods and techniques used by enemy espionage units, and a source of names and identities of enemy agents.

Second, a double agent planted in the intelligence network of any enemy can be used to deceive the enemy. The double agent plants false information to mislead and confuse his superiors, and thereby leads enemy intelligence officers to make wrong conclusions and to move in erroneous directions. The duties of the double agent are among the most dangerous in the field of intelligence.

Intelligence, counterintelligence, espionage, and counter-espionage have been with mankind since earliest time. Reports of these activities are found in the early history of the Hebrew people and of ancient China. During the Jewish Exodus from Egypt to the Promised Land (about 1200 B.C.), according to Numbers 13, "The Lord said to Moses, 'Send men to spy out the land of Canaan, which I give to the people of Israel; from each tribe of their fathers shall you send a man, every one a leader among them.'"

The orders Moses gave his spies were similar to those given to countless agents over the centuries:

Go ... and see what the land is, and whether the people who dwell in it are strong or weak, whether they are few or many, and whether the land that they dwell in is good or bad, and whether the cities that they dwell in are camps or strongholds, and whether the land is rich or poor, and whether there is wood in it or not. Be of good courage, and bring some of the fruit of the land.

After forty days, the author of Numbers tells us, the spies returned, bearing samples of fruit, for, they reported, the land of Canaan "flows with milk and honey." But the spies also reported that "the people who dwell in the land are strong, and the cities are fortified and very large.... We are not able to go up against the people, for they are stronger than we.... The land, through which we have gone, to spy it out is a land that devours its inhabitants; and the people that we saw in it are men of great stature." Thus knowing the strength of their enemies, the Hebrews were able to prepare psychologically and militarily for their invasion of Canaan.

Sun Tzu, an ancient Chinese writer on intelligence problems, sounds almost modern and up to date. In his principal book, *Ping Fa* ("The Art of War"), written about 400 B.C., he describes five kinds of secret agents: agents in place, double agents, deception agents, expendable agents, and penetration agents. "What enables the wise sovereign," Sun Tzu writes, "... to strike and conquer and achieve things beyond the reach of ordinary men, is foreknowledge."

And foreknowledge, he adds, does not come from the gods,

from the study of history, or from "calculations." Foreknowledge comes from secret agents. Sun Tzu gives detailed recommendations on the use of agents and also writes on the techniques of counterespionage, psychological warfare, and the use of deception. Recent Chinese leaders, like Mao Tse-tung, have turned to Sun Tzu's book as a guide for present-day intelligence strategies and tactics.

Intelligence, then, may well be the world's second oldest profession. It plays an essential part in the relations between nations and has done so for so long that most governments have accepted it as a necessary part of existence. Intelligence in Great Britain and France, for instance, is an old and honored profession with a history dating back to the Middle Ages.

With the United States, it has been otherwise. America had no central intelligence organization during peacetime until after World War II. For most of its existence, this country has found no need for large-scale intelligence work. The long history of intelligence in Europe and elsewhere helps explain why it is readily accepted in those countries. The relative newness of intelligence in the United States, on the other hand, helps explain why America has been distrustful of its intelligence organization and at times been highly critical of it.

The Background of Intelligence in the United States

Beginning with the American Revolution, the United States has made use of intelligence, but primarily in time of war. General Washington made use of spies to follow British troop movements and discover the enemy's intentions during the War of Independence.* And during the Civil War, Allan Pinkerton, head of a famous detective agency, helped establish the Secret Service, which set up a network of agents throughout the Confederate States.

---

*One of these spies was Nathan Hale, the first American to be executed by the enemy for intelligence work. Hale was caught by the British on Long Island, where he was making sketches of British troop positions. At his hanging, he was heard by one witness to utter the famous line: "I only regret that I have but one life to lose for my country."

Peacetime intelligence work by the United States, however, was piecemeal and haphazard. In 1793, the Congress granted President Washington the first intelligence contingency fund. The president could use the fund at his discretion and was required to make no public accounting. Washington used the money to finance intelligence work in Spain.

Over the next seventy-five years, other presidents were to follow President Washington's example and send agents to Mexico, Canada, the West Indies, Latin America, Europe, Turkey, Hawaii, the Far East, and elsewhere. But American intelligence in the nineteenth century was very different from today's CIA. No agent made a career of spying. Intelligence was carried out on a part-time basis by businessmen, American travelers abroad, and others, who then returned to their own careers after their mission had been completed. There was no permanent agency to provide training for agents and prepare them for work in the field. Nor had any agency been established to collect and evaluate intelligence on a continuing basis. Intelligence "expertise" was still a thing of the future.

The Secret Service, which continued to exist after the Civil War, was America's first permanent federally funded intelligence agency. During the twenty-five years after the war, according to Rhodri Jeffreys-Jones, whose *American Espionage* (1977) is one of the best books on American intelligence, the Secret Service developed "a professional corps of detectives whose techniques were easily adaptible to the contingencies of espionage." These techniques, Jeffreys-Jones adds, enabled the Secret Service to play an important part in America's first great venture into international affairs at the turn of the century.

By that time, however, the first major controversy over the president's use of intelligence agents had broken out. The dispute arose over America's involvement in Hawaii, which was then an independent chain of islands governed by a monarch. In 1893, President Grover Cleveland sent a special agent, J.H. Blount, to Hawaii to oversee American interests.

A rebellion against the Hawaiian queen, Liliuokalani, soon followed, and the United States annexed the islands in order to restore peace and stability. Secret Commissioner Blount was rumored to have played a covert role in the rebellion against the queen and to have worked for her overthrow. To many Americans of the time, this sort of behavior was unacceptable because it imitated the imperialistic and colonial ambitions of England and France, ambitions which the United States condemned.

One of Blount's most prominent critics was Senator George F. Hoar, a Republican from Massachusetts. Hoar was well known as one of the "anti-imperialists" in the Senate who opposed the American acquisition of colonies. From the floor of the Senate, Hoar declared that the president had the constitutional right to "appoint a mere agent as a messenger, or spy, or a person to gather or convey information."

But, he added, "such a person, so appointed, could be in no sense an officer of the United States." He could "take no office, could exercise no official function, and could do no act whatever which could have any binding force on the United States, or any of the people, merely because he had done it."

Eighty years before the CIA controversies of the 1970s, Hoar had raised one of the most telling criticisms of intelligence work—that secret agents by their work can set off a chain of events that can alter American foreign policy. In this case, the chain of events led to the annexation of Hawaii, without, Hoar believed, proper consultation with the Congress. Such actions undermined the constitutional system of government and placed too much power in the hands of unscrupulous men—the secret agents—who might not feel bound by American legal and political traditions.

During World War I, American intelligence expanded rapidly. The Department of State developed and improved its ability to collect, evaluate, and disseminate information. President Woodrow Wilson, angered by reports of German secret agent activity within the United States, approved the establishment of espionage and counterespionage units.

Some intelligence activity continued after the war. In 1920, a "foreign-intelligence section" was created in the State Department to coordinate intelligence in time of peace. The large-scale efforts of the war years, however, were discontinued and the country lapsed into one of its periods of "isolationism."

The spirit of the times is best conveyed by an action of Secretary of State Henry Stimson. In 1929, Stimson abolished the cryptographic division in the State Department, the unit charged with the breaking of the codes and ciphers of foreign nations. The existence of the division had evidently come as a shock to the secretary of state, for his comment on closing it down was simply, "Gentlemen don't read other people's mail."

Pearl Harbor, World War II, and the OSS

The event that broke America's complacency concerning intelligence was the Japanese attack on Pearl Harbor on December 7, 1941. American intelligence units failed completely to warn of the attack, and the result was disastrous. America's fleet stationed at Pearl Harbor was almost completely destroyed, and the United States was forced to enter World War II in a notably weakened condition.

Could the attack on Pearl Harbor have been prevented by adequate intelligence on the intentions of the Japanese war machine and the movements of its fleets? Most experts believe that it might have been. An official investigation of the attack found that the American Office of Naval Intelligence (ONI) had decoded a Japanese message that revealed plans for an attack on an American target, but could not establish precise details about the attack. This information, however, did not reach the proper authorities.

As the journalist Andrew Tully has pointed out, the attack on Pearl Harbor...

carried a lesson with it to governmental authorities that a nation of America's power and wealth and responsibilities should never have been caught with its guard down. Investigation revealed there had been ample warning that the Japanese were up to something, reams of information picked up here and there that should have alerted Army and Navy commanders in the Pacific that we were in danger. But for the most part this intelligence, gathered by military informants, had lain unused because there was no single, central organization equipped to analyze it and see to its speedy dispatch to those concerned.

[27]

For the United States in 1941, the lesson of Pearl Harbor was clear: if America was going to win World War II, it needed an efficient, well-organized, and effective intelligence organization. But after years of neglect, how could such an organization be built in a short amount of time?

Luckily, President Franklin Roosevelt had been concerned for some time about the outbreak of war. Quietly and secretly, so as not to arouse the suspicions of those who did not want America involved in war, President Roosevelt had begun preparations for the reorganization of American intelligence several months before Pearl Harbor.

The man Roosevelt turned to for help was General William Donovan. General Donovan was an extraordinary man. During World War I, he had earned the name "Wild Bill" as the commander of the "Fighting 69th," and he had won the Congressional Medal of Honor. After the war, Donovan had become a Wall Street lawyer and in the 1930s became an outspoken antifascist who repeatedly warned his fellow countrymen about the aggressive and warlike character of Germany, Italy, and Japan.

Donovan accepted the president's request for help and immediately set about to investigate America's intelligence network and to suggest improvements. He made several trips abroad to acquaint himself with intelligence organizations in foreign countries, particularly Great Britain. On June 10, 1941, six months before Pearl Harbor, Donovan submitted a secret recommendation to Roosevelt entitled "Memorandum of Establishment of Service of Strategic Information."

"Although we are facing imminent peril," Donovan wrote, "we are lacking in effective service for analyzing, comprehending, and appraising such information as we might obtain." Even though intelligence units existed in the Army and Navy, Donovan continued, "our mechanism for collecting information is inadequate" and in need of drastic improvement. He went on to say:

It is essential that we set up a central enemy intelligence organization which would itself collect either directly or through existing departments of government, at home and abroad, pertinent information concerning potential enemies, the character and strength of their armed forces, their internal economic organization, their principal channels of supply, the morale of their troops and their people and their relations with their neighbors or allies.

In his memorandum, Donovan stressed the importance of expertise in intelligence work. The experience of Army and Navy officers is important, he wrote, but of equal importance were the abilities of "specialized trained research officials in the relative scientific fields" such as technology, economics, finance, and psychology. Expert linguists would be needed who could speak a variety of foreign languages. Modern warfare, Donovan added, was "total war" which required "the commitment of all resources of a nation, moral as well as material."

Donovan pointed out two areas of supreme importance in modern intelligence work: economic and psychological warfare. He believed that experts in both areas must be developed and developed quickly. In the field of economic warfare, he said, "there are many weapons that can be used against the enemy" to undermine his economy. But at present, these "weapons" were distributed among many government agencies and without organization or single direction.

Donovan defined psychological warfare as "an attack against the moral and spiritual defenses of a nation." In modern society, he said, the "most powerful weapon" is the radio. He believed that Nazi Germany had perfected the use of the radio to propagandize its own citizens and to demoralize the people of the nations it had conquered.

Donovan also recommended to President Roosevelt that a special intelligence division be established that would conduct clandestine missions behind enemy lines. Units of this division could relay information about enemy strengths and weaknesses and about enemy troop movements and the location of strategic installations. They could also carry out espionage and sabotage and help organize bands of local citizens to resist enemy domination.

President Roosevelt agreed with the policies outlined in Donovan's Memorandum, but told him: "You'll have to start from scratch. We don't have an intelligence service." In July,

1941, Donovan became head of the new Office of the Coordinator of Information (OCI), which was divided the next year, after America's entry into the war, into the Office of Strategic Services (OSS) and the Office of War Information (OWI).

The OSS was Donovan's group. It collected intelligence and carried out programs of economic, psychological, and other forms of "unorthodox" warfare. Teams of scholars and linguists sifted and analyzed information and prepared intelligence reports. Other OSS teams were dropped behind enemy lines, where they prepared the people of the area for the Allied invasion and liberation from Nazi rule.

One of the most remarkable OSS agents was Allen Dulles, who would later serve as a director of the CIA. Dulles was established in Switzerland, a neutral country, to oversee and coordinate intelligence and espionage against Germany. He was a master at his work. He recruited high-level German officials who were willing to serve as double agents in Berlin and carried out many other operations regarded by historians as crucial to the war effort.

But behind the OSS was William Donovan, who served as an extraordinary guide and example for his organization. According to David Bruce, who worked with the OSS and was later ambassador to Great Britain, Donovan's "imagination was unlimited. . . . Ideas were his playthings. Excitement made him snort like a racehorse. Woe to the officer who turned down a project because, on its face, it seemed ridiculous, or at least unusual."

Donovan's imagination was indeed unusual. He entertained, for example, the notion that bats could be used to carry delayed-action incendiary bombs to destroy Tokyo. For Donovan, the plan had considerable merit. The Japanese would not suspect the bats until it was too late, and there would be a minimum loss of American life. He was persuaded, finally, to drop the operation when it became obvious that the bats, which were to come from caves in the western United States, would not survive transportation across the Pacific.

The OSS was the parent organization of the CIA. Many former OSS personnel joined the CIA when it was organized after World War II, and served in important posts in the new Agency. They brought to the CIA the expertise and attitudes they had developed in the OSS—and a firm belief in the importance of intelligence work. The OSS had carried out the largest and most extensive wartime intelligence effort in American history. The CIA was to be the principal part of an even larger intelligence community.

The Creation of the CIA

About six months before the end of World War II, Donovan began to think ahead about America's intelligence needs in the postwar era. In a letter dated 18 November 1944, he outlined his thoughts on a peacetime intelligence organization to President Roosevelt.

"Once our enemies are defeated," Donovan wrote, "the demand will be equally pressing for information that will aid in solving the problems of peace." What this required was "the establishment of a central authority" in the intelligence community that reported directly to the president and which was under the president's direct supervision.

Referring to the OSS, Donovan continued, "We have now in the Government the trained and specialized personnel needed for the task. This talent should not be dispersed" at the conclusion of the war, but should be used to create a peacetime intelligence organization. Donovan attached a page of additional thoughts on a peacetime intelligence organization.

Five months later, on April 5, 1945, President Roosevelt responded favorably to Donovan's suggestions and instructed Donovan to arrange for a meeting of "the chiefs of foreign intelligence and internal security of the various executive agencies, so that a consensus of opinion can be secured." The president, however, died a week later, before any plans for a peacetime central intelligence organization could be prepared.

His successor, Harry Truman, ordered the OSS disbanded on September 20, 1945. At the time, Truman doubted the country's need for a large intelligence organization in time of peace and pointed out that America's intelligence divisions had always been disbanded or cut down after a war's end. Moreover, the new president was under pressure from the FBI, the Army and Navy, the State Department, and the Bureau of the Budget to dissolve the OSS. A peacetime central intelligence organization was unnecessary, these agencies and divisions of government believed, because its duties would overlap with duties they were already in the habit of carrying out.

Truman soon learned, however, that it was difficult to form policy without proper intelligence. Five months after he had dissolved the OSS, on January 22, 1946, he ordered the establishment of a Central Intelligence Group (CIG) and the National Intelligence Authority (NIA).

The CIG was to collect intelligence and report to the NIA, which consisted of the secretaries of state, war, and navy, and their representatives. The NIA would, in turn, advise the president. "Here at last," Truman wrote in his memoirs, "a coordinated method had been worked out, and a practical way had been found for keeping the President informed as to what was known and what was going on."

If President Truman seemed satisfied with the CIG and NIA, many of his advisers were not. Secretary of the Navy James Forrestal believed that the CIG was too weak to carry out the tasks assigned to it. It was constantly mired in bureaucratic quarreling with other government agencies involved in intelligence work, such as the FBI and the intelligence divisions of the State Department and the Army and Navy. It seemed as though no intelligence agency could tolerate the existence of another and that rivalry, bitterness, and confusion were the inevitable curse of America's intelligence network.

Clearly, what was needed was a central intelligence organization with enough power and authority to overcome bureaucratic infighting and establish its own pre-eminence in the intelligence community. Moreover, the need for such an organization was becoming more apparent as time passed. In the years after World War II, tension between the Soviet Union and the United States mounted rapidly. By 1947, the two countries had become bitter enemies, each deeply mistrustful of the other's plans and intentions.

In this atmosphere, many Americans concluded, a strong,

centralized intelligence organization was essential. The United States needed some means to understand Soviet policy and a method to confront Soviet expansion throughout the world. And above all, America needed some way to anticipate—and prevent—a sudden Soviet attack against the United States. No one wanted another Pearl Harbor.

In 1947, the Congress began to hold hearings on the problem of intelligence. Many witnesses were called upon to testify, the most important of whom was probably Allen Dulles, the OSS man who had worked in Switzerland during World War II. During his appearance before the congressional committee, Dulles made several recommendations which later influenced the creation of the CIA.

• Dulles wanted the director of central intelligence to be a civilian, without obligations to the military. He also believed that the intelligence director should have complete authority to choose his own assistants and that a central intelligence organization should control and supervise its own personnel. These suggestions were designed to assure the independence of central intelligence from outside influence.

• Dulles maintained that a central intelligence organization should have control over its budget so that the organization's ability to expand and move in new directions would not be hampered. A government agency with an open budget was an agency that did not have to spend valuable time accounting for its expenditures to Congress. Moreover, a detailed public accounting of intelligence expenditures might prove dangerous, for an enemy could learn from a budget what America's intelligence organization was doing.

• In order to eliminate conflict with other intelligence groups in the government, Dulles suggested that a central intelligence organization should have exclusive supervision over all intelligence operations and access to all intelligence relating to foreign countries. Central intelligence should also be the "recognized authority" to deal with the intelligence organizations of other countries.

[33]

• Dulles wanted central intelligence activity limited to weighing and drawing conclusions. A central intelligence agency, Dulles said, "should have nothing to do with policy. It should try to get at the hard facts on which others must determine policy."

Dulles told the congressional hearings that 80 percent of intelligence could be obtained from open and public sources such as the press and other media of foreign nations and "the many thousands of Americans, business and professional men and American residents of foreign countries, who are naturally brought in touch with what is going on in those countries."

The other 20 percent of intelligence, he said, "is called secret intelligence, namely the intelligence that is obtained by secret means and secret agents." But because of the "glamor and mystery" that surrounds the work of secret agents, he added, too much emphasis is placed on secret intelligence when open intelligence is actually far more important.

• Finally, Dulles recommended that intelligence work become a career in which men and women spend their lives after rigorous training. "Service in the Agency," he emphasized, "should not be viewed merely as a steppingstone to promotion in one of the armed services or other branches of the Government." And an "official secrets" act should be passed that would make intelligence personnel punishable if they violated national security.

Dulles took British intelligence as an example to be imitated. "The British system," he pointed out, "has behind it a long history of quiet and effective performance, based on a highly trained personnel with years of service and great technical ability." In the United States, he concluded, "we have the raw material for building the greatest intelligence service in the world. But to accomplish this we must make it a respected, continuing, and adequately remunerated career."

Dulles argued that the personnel of a central intelligence organization "need not be very numerous" and, in a phrase that is often quoted in histories of the CIA, he declared that an ideal intelligence service "should be directed by a relatively small but elite corps of men with a passion for anonymity and a willingness to stick at the particular job."

As a result of the hearings, Congress passed the National Security Act of 1947, which was signed into law by President Truman. The act created the CIA out of the earlier CIG and listed five "powers and duties" of the Central Intelligence Agency. These powers and duties gave the CIA broad authority in the collection, evaluation, and dissemination of intelligence pertaining to national security.

The act placed several restrictions on the new Agency. It was to have "no police, subpoena, law-enforcement powers, or internal security functions," which meant that it could not legally operate within the United States. These restrictions were added to prevent the CIA from becoming a secret police force and to make certain that its work would not overlap with that of the FBI. The CIA was to turn its attention abroad and leave domestic matters to the Federal Bureau of Investigation.

The most general power and duty granted the CIA by the National Security Act of 1947 was the fifth. It stated that it was the Agency's responsibility "to perform such other functions and duties related to intelligence affecting the national security as the National Security Council may from time to time direct."

The wording of the law—which gave the CIA the right to carry out "such other functions and duties related to intelligence"—seemed very broad and was used by Agency officials to justify a wide range of CIA activities. The law, however, is not the blank check it first appears to be. It requires the Agency to carry out its activities *only* at the direction of the National Security Council, whose membership includes the president, vice-president, the secretaries of state and defense, and other high officials. The National Security Council, therefore, was to have a veto power over the CIA and the authority to halt Agency operations it did not approve.

Two years after the National Security Act, Congress added to the powers and independence of the CIA by the passage of the Central Intelligence Agency Act of 1949. This act gave the director of central intelligence (DCI) almost complete freedom from civil service regulations in the hiring and firing of CIA employees. This made it possible for the DCI to organize the Agency and discipline its membership without outside interference.

But more importantly, the Central Intelligence Agency Act of 1949 granted the Agency an extraordinary degree of financial independence. It exempted the CIA from any responsibility to publish or disclose the "functions, names, official titles, salaries or numbers of personnel employed." And it directed the Bureau of the Budget (now the Office of Management and Budget, or OMB) to make no reports to the Congress on these matters.

Moreover, the DCI was given the right to spend funds from the CIA's annual appropriation on his personal voucher, which meant that he did not have to account in detail for the money spent by the CIA. The DCI could turn to the annual appropriation "for objects of a confidential, extraordinary, or emergency nature." And since the Agency's budget soon grew to be very large, this law gave the CIA director the power to distribute enormous sums of money in order to finance the CIA's projects throughout the world.

The financial independence and freedom Congress granted the CIA director is almost unheard of in the history of American government. Intelligence expert Harry Howe Ransom calls it "truly an extraordinary power for the head of any Executive agency." The Congress, however, was firmly convinced that these unusual measures were necessary in order to assure the utmost secrecy at the CIA—and to make certain the Agency was strong and wealthy enough to meet communist expansion and activity wherever it might arise.

The National Security Act of 1947 and the Central Intelligence Agency Act of 1949 provided the basis for a powerful, centralized Agency to oversee American intelligence in the cold war. As time passed, CIA practice was revised and often improved by recommendations from the DCI or by executive order from the president. And on occasion presidents used their power to appoint special "watchdog" committees to look into intelligence work and offer suggestions for change.

A 1954 report drawn up by one such committee reveals the high degree of fear and concern the cold war had created in the United States. It also helps to explain why American officials decided to place so much power and authority in the hands of the CIA.

Owing to the present-day world situation, the report declared, the United States may have to adopt tactics "more ruthless" than those "employed by the enemy."

> *It is now clear that we are facing an implacable enemy whose avowed objective is world domination by whatever means at whatever cost. There are no rules in such a game. Hitherto acceptable norms of human conduct do not apply. If the United States is to survive, long standing American concepts of American fair play must be reconsidered.*

The report also emphasized the necessity of "an aggressive covert psychological, political, and paramilitary organization"—the CIA—that would be "far more effective" and "more unique" than enemy intelligence organizations. "No one," the report concluded, "should be permitted to stand in the way of the prompt, efficient, and secure accomplishment of this mission."

These statements indicate the regard enjoyed by the CIA during its formation and early years. A child of the cold war, it was nutured by fond and anxious parents—the Congress and the president—who looked upon it as an essential element in the future well-being of the country. In this atmosphere, the CIA grew rapidly and vigorously, and, the critics would add, became more than a bit spoiled and far too convinced of its own importance.

CHAPTER THREE

THE CIA
IN ACTION

*"There were so many CIA projects
at the height of the Cold War
that it was almost impossible for
a man to keep them in balance."*

**Tom Braden, political commentator
and former CIA division chief**

By 1948 most of the nations of Eastern Europe had communist governments and were allies of the Soviet Union. In 1949 the Chinese forces under Mao Tse-Tung defeated the nationalist army, and China too became a communist country. Communist guerrillas were active in Greece, Turkey, and Southeast Asia. In France and Italy, large and well-organized communist parties seemed to threaten democratic societies.

Throughout the world, communism appeared to be on the rise and to offer hope to nations devastated by World War II, or to colonial peoples in Africa and Asia who longed to be independent. Democracy, on the other hand, appeared to be on the defensive. It was in these circumstances that the CIA began its work and was charged with the responsibility of containing communism and defending American interests.

The Early CIA
Thomas Powers, author of the informative *The Man Who Kept the Secrets; Richard Helms & the CIA* (1979), describes "three distinct types of personality" that characterized employees of the CIA from the beginning. These three personality types correspond to the three general types of activity per-

formed by the Agency: the "spy runners," the "analysts," and the "political operators."

The chief characteristics of the spy runners, Powers says, are "discretion, restraint, and exactitude." Their work is "equally divided between the penetration and preservation of secrets." They are the traditional spies, whose work requires that they cultivate "invisibility" and the most rigid discipline. The spy runners have the advantage of gathering intelligence in the field and on the scene.

The analysts, on the other hand, have a "glutton's appetite for paper" and for "anything at all which can be written down, stacked on a desk, and read." They can work at CIA headquarters, far removed from the hurly-burly of political life, with information gleaned from foreign radio broadcasts, published journals and newspapers, and reports from the field.

The analysts, Powers points out, base their work on two assumptions. First, they believe that the enemy is consistent and rational, and that his future behavior can be predicted from his past behavior. Second, they assume that the enemy will not take any undue risks, unless he has something to gain by his risks. Without these two assumptions, Powers claims, the analysts would be hard-pressed to make accurate forecasts of future situations. Their work is complex enough, without the added annoyance that behavior is not always rational or efficient and that men often take risks that seem unreasonable.

The third personality type, the political or covert operators, are, in Powers' words, the "adventurers" of the Agency. They are "aggressive" and "enthusiastic," but "too often morally careless." They look upon the world as "infinitely plastic" and believe they can "do anything with funds and a broad okay from the top."

The political operators also tend to be optimistic and full of self-confidence, "convinced that every problem has its handle, and that the CIA could find a way to reach it." If the chief qualities of the spy are restraint and discipline and those of the analyst an addiction to paperwork and reasoning, then those of the political operator are the ability to come up with many "bright ideas" on how an operation might be carried out and a willingness to try anything to get a job done.

[41]

Each of the three groups was active during the early years of the CIA. CIA spies were present in Western Europe and attempted to penetrate the Soviet Union and its satellites. Attempts were likewise made to place agents in communist China. The penetration of communist countries, however, proved very difficult and was successful only in rare instances. Such endeavors were later abandoned for more fruitful work.

One of the first CIA efforts in Western Europe involved the establishment of "stay-behind networks" in countries believed to be under the threat of Soviet attack. These networks were made up of men and women trained by American agents to go underground in the event of a Soviet attack and be ready to carry out sabotage and espionage when the time came.

From the beginning, CIA analysts made every effort to see that the collection of intelligence was as thorough and effective as possible. Radio broadcasts in the Soviet Union, its satellite states, and communist China were monitored and transcribed. Soviet and Chinese books, magazines, newspapers, and other publications were carefully read and analyzed. The numerous refugees fleeing communist countries were interviewed, as were Western travelers and businessmen who made visits behind the "iron curtain."

Out of this enormous and disorganized body of information, the analysts made files on every aspect of communist activity. Personality profiles were written up on Soviet leaders, enemy agents, communist party members, and anyone else active in communist political life and society. These files contained physical descriptions, biographical sketches, and personal information, such as weaknesses or flaws that could be exploited. An enemy agent, for instance, with a known love for money and high living, was possibly an agent who could be bribed to give intelligence to the United States.

On many occasions, agents in the field and analysts found their work complementary. No source of intelligence could be ignored, because valuable information could be gleaned from unusual places. In Vienna, for example, a CIA agent came into possession of the trash that had been taken from a Russian commercial airliner. When he went through the trash, he discovered, among other things, a bent coat hanger, which he carefully wrapped and sent off to Washington.

CIA analysts were able to learn much from the hanger. For several months, they had known of the existence of a new Soviet long-range bomber, but did not know its range or the bomb load it could carry. What they did know, however, was that metal shavings from the bomber's wing were saved and melted down to make coat hangers. The coat hanger from Vienna proved to be made from these shavings and by spectroanalysis and chemical tests, the experts learned the kind of metal used to make the long-range bomber's wing. Knowledge of the type of metal allowed the specialists to determine the stress and tension the plane was designed to withstand. From this data, it was only a few steps before the range and bomb load capacity of the Soviet plane were discovered.

The political operators, or "adventurers," as Powers calls them, were full of plans and operations. There was a great hope that the "Soviet empire"—the USSR and its satellites and communist China—would prove vulnerable to internal upheaval and turmoil. With this in mind, the CIA trained refugees from communist countries to return to their homelands as secret agents. These agents were to locate anticommunists, organize them into teams, carry out sabotage and espionage, and await liberation from communist rule.

The CIA also gave aid and support to anticommunist guerrilla bands in the Ukraine, where they waged a futile war against Soviet oppression. An attempt was made to organize an anticommunist guerrilla band in Albania. And in the Far East, the Agency recruited nationalist Chinese from the island of Taiwan to return to the mainland for intelligence missions.

CIA political operatives established the International Organizations Division of the Agency (IOD), headed by Tom Braden and his deputy, Cord Meyer* The IOD's responsibility was to help organize and support free labor unions, free student societies, the Congress of Cultural Freedom, and a series of other organizations of veterans, lawyers, and others.

---

*As has been mentioned, Braden is now a well-known Washington commentator. Cord Meyer likewise has left the CIA for journalism and now writes a syndicated column that appears in many newspapers. Both men are well-informed sources of information on the CIA.

These organizations under IOD sponsorship were to represent democratic ideals and other Western traditions. Their duty was to attract the loyalties of their members away from communism and to serve as opposition groups to groups organized and supported by the communists. If a viable, attractive alternative to communism was offered, the argument behind the creation of the IOD ran, then communism would lose its power to attract new followers.

An additional effort in the field of propaganda was made by the CIA by the establishment of Radio Free Europe and Radio Liberty. Radio Free Europe regularly broadcast programs and information to the nations of Eastern Europe in the various native languages; Radio Liberty broadcast to the Soviet Union. Both stations sought to give people behind the iron curtain news they would not otherwise have and to propagandize the Western view of the cold war.

The CIA in Italy
American officials, and especially CIA analysts, found the post–World War II situation in Italy disturbing. Italian society and economic life had been profoundly weakened by the war. Moreover, the Italian Communist Party (PCI) was the largest communist party outside of the Soviet Union and the communist world and was playing an important and active role in Italian life.

Under the able leadership of Palmiro Togliatti, the PCI was expanding its membership and cementing close ties with labor unions, student groups, and numerous other organizations. PCI activities were heavily funded by the Soviet Union, and many observers believed that it stood a good chance to equal, and perhaps overtake, Italy's more moderate parties in the elections scheduled for 1948.

At the first meeting of the National Security Council on December 19, 1947, it was decided to allow the CIA to operate in Italy. Admiral Roscoe Hillenkoetter, the CIA director, turned responsibility for the Agency's work in Italy over to a division of the CIA known as the Office of Special Operations (OSO). On December 22, the OSO set up the Special Procedures Group (SPG) to direct the effort.

The Special Procedures Group carried out a program of political and psychological warfare for the minds of Italian voters. CIA funds were used to pay for the printing of posters and pamphlets to advertise candidates of centrist parties and to strengthen the position of moderates. Parties of the far right and the far left were targeted for defeat. The Agency looked with particular approval on the Christian Democrats, a party of moderates, conservatives, and liberals united by their Catholic faith and their belief in democracy. The Christian Democrats, it was believed, stood the best chance of winning.

Much of the propaganda financed by the CIA was "white" propaganda—the simple truth about the candidates and the political situation. But some of it fell under the name "disinformation," which ex-CIA employee Victor Marchetti calls "the spreading of false information in order to influence people's opinions or actions." CIA agents forged documents and letters that purported to come from the Italian Communist Party, letters and documents that were designed to put the PCI in a bad light and to discredit Communist leaders.

The Agency also paid for the publication of anonymous books and magazine articles that told in vivid detail about communist activities in Eastern Europe and the Soviet Union. These works stressed such incidents as the looting and destruction of East Germany by Soviet troops at the end of World War II. Others described communist seizures of power in formerly democratic countries, implying that a similar fate might await Italy.

The Christian Democrats won the elections of 1948, gaining nearly half the seats in the Italian parliament. The Communists came in a poor second. Some commentators believe that the Christian Democrats could have won without CIA help, but the Agency looked upon its effort as significant and believed that it had not only played a positive role in the 1948 elections, but also had begun to lay a groundwork for the continued development of a strong democratic and moderate force in Italian politics.

The experience, and successes, of the CIA's Special Procedures Group in Italy helped to whet the American appetite for political covert action operations. A high-ranking official in the State Department recommended that an organization be established to do for the whole world what the SPG had done in Italy. And in June, 1948, the National Security Council authorized the establishment of just such a group, which it named the Office of Policy Coordination.

The NSC directive creating the OPC defined its responsibilities as

propaganda, economic warfare: preventive direct action, including sabotage, antisabotage, demolition and evacuation measures; subversion against hostile states, including assistance to underground resistance groups, and support of indigenous anti-Communist elements in threatened countries of the free world.

The directive likewise said that the OPC was to direct its operations toward the "vicious covert activities of the USSR, its satellite countries and Communist groups" and to prevent their efforts "to discredit the aims and activities of the United States and other Western powers." The NSC directive warned, however, that the OPC was to conduct its operations so "that any U.S. government responsibility for them is not evident to unauthorized persons and that if uncovered the U.S. government can plausibly disclaim any responsibility for them."

The OPC soon became the most rapidly growing section of the CIA. By the end of its first year, it had 300 employees and seven overseas field stations. Three years later, it had 2,812 full-time people, forty-seven overseas stations, and its budget had grown from $4.7 million per year to $82 million.

CIA involvement in the political life of Italy did not end with the elections of 1948. The Communists had been defeated but were still a very strong party which received an estimated $50 million a year in aid from the Soviet Union. Moreover, Italian politics were known to be volatile and highly changeable. The force that gave the Christian Democrats the victory in 1948 might shift and bring the PCI to victory in the next elections.

CIA aid continued to support the Christian Democrats and moderate political candidates. Pamphlets, posters, and other propaganda materials were financed, and assistance was given in staging political congresses and rallies and in conducting voter-registration campaigns. In addition, Agency help was given in strengthening noncommunist labor unions, in building competitive democratic worker cooperatives, and in establishing cultural, civic, and political groups—all areas where the Italian Communist Party had moved earlier and gained a lead over moderate parties.

William Colby, later a director of central intelligence, worked in Italy during this period for the OPC. In his autobiography, *Honorable Men: My Life in the CIA* (1978), Colby discusses OPC activity in Italy and defends its achievements. "I believe ...," Colby writes, "[that the OPC in Italy] showed that the long-term strategy of covert political help to democratic forces can work and can frustrate the hopes of authoritarians to capture democratic voters for a nondemocratic cause."

The success of the OPC operation in Italy, Colby continues, "cannot be used to justify every CIA intervention abroad." But it can, he maintains, be used to demonstrate the "utility" and "morality" of such operations. The OPC operation in Italy helped to undermine communist subversion in a nation friendly to the United States. By settling Italian problems at a political level, the Agency made a military solution unnecessary. The American armed forces, Colby implies, did not have to liberate Italy from communist rule because the CIA had stopped the communists at the polls.

The CIA mission in Italy was only one of several similar operations during the early years of the Agency. OPC activities of a comparable nature were carried out in France, West Germany, and elsewhere. As time passed, and more came to be known about these secret and clandestine political operations, critics denounced the CIA for its interference in the internal affairs of other countries.

For those in the CIA, however, and for many other government officials, Italy was proof that covert political action worked and worked well, if properly funded and managed. The CIA experience in Italy served as a model for CIA work in other countries.

The CIA and the Korean War

The Korean War touched off one of the earliest controversies surrounding the CIA. The Agency was charged with a "massive intelligence failure" and ineptitude because it had not anticipated the North Korean attack on South Korea which came on June 24, 1950. Official Washington began to wonder if the CIA were capable of living up to its responsibilities.

The charge was unfair. For almost a year, the CIA had noted a buildup of North Korean troops along the South Korean border and had predicted an invasion of the South. Warnings had been sent to the proper American authorities. What the Agency failed to do, CIA Director Hillenkoetter explained to a congressional committee, was to predict the *exact* date of the invasion and this, he pointed out, was a very difficult thing to do.*

Unfair or not, however, the charge stuck, and for many members of Congress and others, it offered proof that the CIA was in need of an overhaul. Hillenkoetter retired and was replaced by General Walter Bedell Smith, a man of extraordinary administrative abilities who had been General Eisenhower's chief of staff during World War II. Smith set out immediately to improve the CIA from top to bottom, emphasizing the Agency's estimating and forecasting capabilities.

Smith has been described by a close friend as "a man of decisive action." He was largely self-educated and had never attended college. He served in both World Wars, rising to the rank of general in 1942. After World War II, he was appointed ambassador to the Soviet Union. He was to serve only two and a half years as CIA director, but he nevertheless managed to leave a strong imprint of his personality and ideas on the Agency and its activities.

As a young man, Smith had wanted to make a career of

---

*Later in the Korean War, the CIA was charged with failing to warn General Douglas MacArthur, the commander of the UN forces, that large numbers of Chinese communist troops were about to enter the war on the side of the North Koreans. This charge too was unfair. The CIA warned about the Chinese troops, but General MacArthur appears to have ignored the warning.

army intelligence. When he applied for a position, however, he was told that army intelligence was largely the work of military attachés at foreign embassies, who were expected to be wealthy enough to wine and dine those people that might have information the United States needed. Smith was a man of modest means with no private income and had to abandon his hopes for work in intelligence. As director of the CIA, one of his chief concerns became the establishment of a first-rate training program for CIA agents who wanted to make a career in the intelligence community.

Earlier CIA training programs for junior agents had been disorganized and divided among the divisions of the Agency. A few CIA divisions had no training programs at all. Under Smith, the training of new recruits became centralized in the Office of Training. Only the best candidates were accepted, and an elaborate screening process was developed to weed out applicants who proved undesirable.

If the applicant passed the rigorous initial examinations, his first year with the CIA was passed in formal training. This was followed by assignments in various divisions of the Agency for two more years. Altogether, the junior agent spent three years under the guidance of the Office of Training before he was given a permanent assignment.

Smith also turned his attention toward the research divisions of the CIA. When he came to the Agency, Smith found these divisions large, unwieldy, and uncoordinated. He left them better organized and better staffed. He oversaw the establishment of an office to handle current intelligence which was to keep abreast of world developments twenty-four hours a day and produce succinct, well-written summaries of them.

He likewise created the Office of National Estimates (ONE) and staffed it with the best minds he could find from the ambassador corps, the academic world, business, law, and the military. Rather than concern itself with day-to-day affairs, the staff of ONE was to deal with what might happen in the future on a country by country basis. Experts on Brazil, for instance, would deal with Brazil; experts on the Soviet Union would deal with the Soviet Union.

Smith's reorganization of the CIA helped to produce a more tightly knit and efficient organization. His achievements have been highly regarded by many historians of the Agency. Lyman Kirkpatrick, who worked with Smith at the CIA writes:

General Bedell Smith headed the CIA at a crucial period in its history. The Korean War was the final blow needed to force the United States to revitalize its defense establishment and to build a modern intelligence system. If the CIA was to survive the bureaucratic battles and emerge as the strong keystone of the federal intelligence structure, it was at this time that it needed a powerful hand at the helm. Smith had what was needed.

CHAPTER FOUR

THE CIA IN IRAN AND GUATEMALA

*"Where there begins to be evidence
that a country is slipping and
Communist takeover is threatened...
we can't wait for an engraved invitation
to come and give aid."*

CIA Director Allen Dulles

General Smith left the Agency in February, 1952, and was replaced by Allen Dulles, whom he had brought to the CIA to serve as his deputy. Dulles was the first CIA director to come to his job with broad intelligence experience; during World War II he had conducted the OSS operation in Berne, Switzerland, and earned a reputation as a master spy.

Under Dulles, the Agency was to achieve some of its greatest successes, as well as experience its most discouraging failure. It was likewise to undergo rapid growth. In 1950, the CIA had about 5,000 employees. By 1955, it had about 15,000, and had recruited many contract employees and foreign agents.

During the same period, the Agency began to show greater interest in the countries of the third world. The poor and underdeveloped nations of Latin America, Africa, and Asia offered fertile ground for the growth of communism. And it was there, many Washington policy makers believed, that one of the most important cold war struggles between the United States and the Soviet Union would be played out.

The CIA in Iran
One country closely watched by CIA analysts was Iran. On the north, Iran was bordered by the Soviet Union. In 1946, the

Soviet Union had attempted to establish a puppet communist government in the Iranian province of Azerbaijan, but the government had been expelled by force. Communist influence in Iran, however, remained significant, and there was a small, but active communist party.

Iran was ruled by Shah Mohammed Reza Pahlavi. The young Shah was popular in his country, but was also widely regarded as a playboy whose ability to govern was untested and who might prove unable to rule forcefully. A serious test of the Shah's ability appeared in 1950 and 1951, when a rising surge of nationalist feeling in Iran forced him to appoint as premier a widely admired politician, Mohammed Mossadegh.

Mossadegh took office on April 28, 1951. A man of more than seventy years, he was given to weeping in public and to frequent complaints of serious illness. He was nevertheless a man who had a program to carry out in Iran. Mossadegh had enormous contempt for the Pahlavi dynasty, which he regarded as unconstitutional. His efforts as premier, therefore, were directed against the Shah, to weaken the Shah's authority and isolate him from the nation.

Mossadegh forced Princess Ashraf, the Shah's twin sister, into exile. He had an investigation begun into the Pahlavi family's enormous wealth, which he believed had been illegally obtained. And he began to remove pro-Shah elements from the Iranian army and replace them with troops loyal to the premier.

But Mossadegh's most daring move was the nationalization of the Anglo-Iranian Oil Company (AIOC), a British-owned petroleum concern, and one of the world's largest oil refineries at Abadan on the Persian Gulf. Nationalization was welcomed by many Iranians, but it was a step that angered the West. Great Britain boycotted Iran, and the United States joined the British in condemning Mossadegh and in refusing to purchase Iranian oil.

The West might have waited for Mossadegh's government to fall as a result of financial collapse due to the lost oil revenues, had not another problem arisen. Western intelligence sources reported that the premier was carrying on a secret relationship with the Tudeh, Iran's communist party. In addition, these sources likewise reported the presence of numerous Soviet intelligence personnel in Iran, several of whom were in direct contact with Mossadegh.

The reaction to this information in Washington was deep concern. The West simply could not tolerate the loss of another country—and particularly the loss of Iran—to the Soviet Union. On May 28, 1953, Mossadegh sent a letter to President Eisenhower that challenged the United States to give aid to Iran or Iran would turn "elsewhere" for help. By elsewhere, he meant the Soviet Union.

A CIA plan for Iran, however, was already in the works. CIA analysts had come to the conclusion that although Mossadegh had great popularity, he had never succeeded in undermining the warmth many Iranians felt for the Shah. The problem, then, was to bolster the authority of the Shah while weakening that of Mossadegh.

The responsibility for the CIA mission in Iran fell to Kermit "Kim" Roosevelt, the Agency's chief operative in the Middle East. Roosevelt, thirty-seven, was the grandson of President Theodore Roosevelt and had taught history at Harvard, his alma mater, before working for the OSS in World War II. He was a man of broad experience and imagination and was regarded as one of the Agency's best agents.

Sometime during the summer of 1953, Roosevelt entered Iran legally by driving across the border from Iraq. He drove to Teheran, where he immediately went underground. In the next few weeks, Roosevelt was careful to move his headquarters from time to time to elude Mossadegh's agents. He was assisted by CIA agents already in Iran and by Iranian agents, with whom he kept in touch through intermediaries. Roosevelt carried CIA funds to finance his operation.

About the same time, another American, Brigadier General H. Norman Schwartzkopf, entered Iran. Schwartzkopf appears not to have been a CIA employee, but nevertheless played a part in the Agency's plans for Iran. The general knew the country well. Between 1942 and 1948, he had been in charge of restructuring the Shah's national police force. He had many powerful friends in Iran, including Major General Fazlollah Zahedi of the Iranian army, who had once served as Iran's minister of the interior.

Unlike Roosevelt, Schwartzkopf remained open. He visited his old friends and may have had a hand in bringing the crisis in Iran to a head. On August 13, 1953, not long after Schwartzkopf's arrival in Iran, the Shah found the courage to sign a decree that ousted Mossadegh from power. The decree also announced that General Zahedi, Schwartzkopf's close friend, would become the new premier.

Events now began to move quickly. Mossadegh refused to recognize the decree and arrested the officer who had brought it to him. Anti-Shah mobs took to the streets in Teheran and rioting ensued, led by supporters of Mossadegh and by communists. In the chaos, the Shah and his wife fled by plane to Baghdad and then to Rome.

For four days, the pro-Mossadegh mobs controlled the capital. Statues of the Shah were torn down and destroyed. The political climate of Iran was tense. But then, on August 19, a sudden change occurred. The army, whose loyalties had always been in question, began to round up and arrest pro-Mossadegh demonstrators.

From his underground headquarters, Kim Roosevelt ordered his American and Iranian agents to carry out their mission. Roosevelt's program was political warfare at its best and most imaginative. He had arranged for a pro-Shah demonstration to take place, and now, he believed, was the right time for the demonstration.

Roosevelt's demonstrators were a motley crew of performers—tumblers, weight lifters, musclemen, wrestlers, boxers, and gymnasts—who would easily catch the eyes of onlookers. The demonstrators wound their way through the streets of Teheran and at a prearranged signal began to shout "Long live the Shah!" and "Death to Mossadegh!" Other pro-Shah Iranians swelled the ranks of the parade.

A brief skirmish followed, in which troops loyal to the Shah fought with troops that remained loyal to Mossadegh. Before midnight, however, the premier's soldiers were forced to surrender after they had been driven into a narrow circle around Mossadegh's palace. The premier was found inside and arrested. The Shah and his wife returned from Rome in triumph.

The CIA operation in Iran, by Agency standards, had been a success. A man regarded as dangerous to American interests had been deposed and had been replaced by the Shah, whose friendship for the United States was considered firm. The operation, too, had moved quickly and efficiently, and CIA involvement had been concealed. But most important, Soviet influence in Iran had been greatly diminished and the threat of a communist take-over had been removed.

The CIA in Guatemala

In 1944, a student revolt overthrew longtime Guatemalan dictator Jorge Ubico, and Juan José Arevalo, a socialist, became president in elections held the following year. Arevalo was strongly anti-American, but a cautious reformer. He began to pave the way for a land reform program that would turn over the property of Guatemala's few enormously wealthy landholders to the poor and dispossessed.

Arevalo's successor, Jacobo Arbenz Guzmán, hoped to complete the program. Arbenz became president in March, 1951. By June, 1952, he had pushed a land reform bill through the Guatemalan legislature. The program was moderate in scope and called for "the development of the peasant capitalist economy and the capitalist agriculture in general."

But moderate or not, the program alienated those who already held land, from the owners of great estates to the small landowners. It likewise angered the American-owned United Fruit Company, whose land holdings in Guatemala were among the largest. Under the land reform program, only lands in disuse were to be expropriated, and the Arbenz government expropriated 225,000 acres (91,125 ha) of idle United Fruit Company property to distribute among landless peasants.

In order to gain support for his controversial program, Arbenz turned increasingly to the Guatemalan left and to Guatemalan communists. Arbenz claimed not to be a communist, and communist writers refer to him as a "bourgeois reformist." But whatever his true political affiliation, by 1954 observers noted the presence of communists in key positions throughout the government, and many believed that Guatemala was rapidly moving into the Soviet orbit.

Evidence of communist activity in Guatemala came from a number of sources, but one of the most startling examples came from a series of discoveries by CIA agents working in Europe, Africa, and the Caribbean area. The story is told by the journalist Andrew Tully in his book *CIA: The Inside Story* (1962). In Tully's words, "the Guatemala story shows CIA at its very best—in the gathering of information world-wide, in the communication of that information to headquarters and in its speedy evaluation for the guidance of policy makers."

The story began in Szczecin, a port city in communist Poland. A German businessman, who was also a secret CIA agent, noticed activities which he thought might interest the Agency. The German managed a small machine-tool factory, and his intelligence work was unknown to Polish authorities. In order to get his information out of Poland, he dictated a letter to his secretary, who was also a CIA agent. The letter was purely businesslike, but concealed under one period was a piece of microfilm on which the businessman and his secretary had placed the information.

After being approved by an unsuspecting Polish official, the letter was mailed to Paris. In Paris, it arrived at a CIA "drop," an address regularly used by the Agency for its operations. It was picked up by another businessman, also a CIA agent, who took it to a photographic studio. In the back room of the shop, a CIA microfilm expert examined the letter, scraping at each period with a razor until one period fell off.

The small piece of microfilm, not much larger than the head of a pin, was enlarged so it could be read—but not understood, for it was in code. A CIA radio operator then transmitted the message by shortwave to Washington under the words: "For AWD's Eyes Only." AWD referred to Allen Dulles, the CIA director, whose office held the key that would break the code.

The message said that the freighter *Alfhem,* flying the flag of Sweden, had been loaded in Szczecin with 15,000 crates and boxes that contained munitions from the Skoda armament works in Czechoslovakia. This was the activity noticed by the German businessman/CIA agent in Poland. The message also said that the businessman had heard unconfirmed reports that the ship was heading for a port in the western hemisphere.

Radio messages were sent out to CIA agents in port cities in Europe and Africa. It was learned that the *Alfhem* was bound for Dakar in French West Africa (now Senegal) with a load of optical laboratory equipment. From Dakar, however, came word that the freighter changed course before reaching Africa and was now bound for Trujillo, Honduras. Caribbean CIA agents reported that the *Alfhem's* real destination was Puerto Barrios in Guatemala. And on May 15, agents in Guatemala noted the arrival of the ship and the unloading of its cargo.

The implications of all this intelligence were obvious. Communist aid had arrived in Guatemala in the form of armaments that would be used to strengthen the Arbenz government and lead to a communist or at least openly pro-Soviet regime in Latin America. Alarmed, Allen Dulles called a meeting of the National Security Council to warn that the arms shipment threatened not only Guatemala, but all of Central America, including the Panama Canal.

The news convinced the president and his advisers, as well as CIA officials, that something had to be done, and done quickly. For several months the Agency had been preparing a plan of action for Guatemala, and now was clearly the time for the plan to be put into effect.

The CIA's plan involved several stages. First, the Agency had selected a nationally known figure who could replace Arbenz once he had been deposed. Not anyone would do. He had to be politically acceptable to the CIA and dependable. And he had to be a man who would quickly gain the support of Guatemalans, and particularly the Guatemalan army.

The Agency settled on Colonel Carlos Castillo Armas. Castillo was a prominent figure among anti-Arbenz Guatemalans. He had led a revolt against Arbenz three years earlier, and when he was imprisoned, had tunneled his way to freedom, escaping Guatemala for asylum elsewhere in Central America. Furthermore, Castillo was familiar with the United States and had spent two years at the U.S. Army Command and General Staff School at Ft. Leavenworth, Kansas.

With CIA help, Castillo set up his headquarters in Tegucigalpa, the capital of Honduras. On Momotombito, a volcanic island in Nicaragua, a camp was established. It was there that the troops Castillo would use in an invasion of Guatemala were trained and prepared. The training was under the supervision of a CIA official who went under the name of "Colonel Rutherford."

The CIA also supplied air support for the invasion in the form of P-47 Thunderbolts and C-47 transports that operated out of Managua, Nicaragua's capital city. The pilots of the planes were Americans hired by the Agency.

When the *Alfhem* docked at Puerto Barrios on May 15, the Guatemalan operation began to move to a climax. Two days later, the State Department made public the presence of Soviet arms in Guatemala, and five days after that, Washington began to send arms and ammunition to Nicaragua. The arms shipments to Nicaragua, the State Department declared, were a "countermeasure" to the communist shipments to Guatemala. What is more likely is that the arms were to be used by Castillo's troops.

On June 18, Colonel Castillo led his small Army of Liberation across the Guatemalan border from Honduras and occupied the small town of Esquipulas, near the Pacific coast. On the first day of the invasion, CIA planes dropped propaganda leaflets on Guatemala City, urging the people of the capital to overthrow the Arbenz regime and welcome Colonel Castillo and his men. Behind the scenes, the American ambassador to Guatemala, John Peurifoy, began to work for the establishment of a government friendly to the United States. Back in Esquipulas, the colonel brought the invasion to a momentary halt, waiting for the government to fall.

During the next week, the P-47's strafed the capital city. But then a snag occurred in the operation. Three of the planes were lost in accidents, and without these planes, the mission was in danger of failure. Allen Dulles made an urgent appeal to President Eisenhower for more planes. Eisenhower agreed but insisted that the planes be sold to Nicaragua by the American Air Force in order to conceal American participation in the invasion. Nicaragua could then turn the planes over to the rebels.

Meanwhile, at the United Nations, Guatemala accused the United States of complicity in the invasion. But Henry Cabot Lodge, the American ambassador to the UN, denied the charge categorically. "The situation," he stated, "does not involve aggression but is a revolt of Guatemalans against Guatemalans."

The strafing of Guatemala City and other important urban areas continued. By June 24, it was clear that Arbenz was losing his nerve. Colonel Rodolfo Mendoza Azurdia, the head of the Guatemalan Air Force, defected to Colonel Castillo. Arbenz could no longer count on the loyalty of other officers. Commanders on the front sent back messages which said that their forces were being overwhelmed by the invaders. The reports were not true and were intended to demoralize the president and bring about his resignation.

CIA agents in Guatemala exploited the chaos for the benefit of the Agency. Clandestine radio operators intercepted radio communications and then sent out false and misleading messages on the same wavelength. On June 25, a P-47 dropped a bomb on Guatemala City, and two days later, June 27, Arbenz surrendered.

On July 3, Colonel Castillo entered Guatemala City triumphantly. During the week that followed, he was elected president. His government acted quickly to put a halt to the land reform program and eventually took more than 800,000 acres (324,000 ha) of land from peasants and returned it to its original owners. Rigid anticommunist laws were passed, and people suspected of leftist leanings or activities were arrested and imprisoned.

As it did in the Iranian operation, the CIA looked upon its work in Guatemala as a success. A government friendly to the United States had been established, and the Agency had shown that it could handle a variety of problems, including political warfare, the training of rebel troops, and the outfitting of a small air force. Because of its success, the CIA operation in Guatemala served as a model for later, more elaborate operations undertaken by the Agency.

CHAPTER FIVE

THE U-2 INCIDENT: SUCCESS AND CONTROVERSY

"We'll never be able to match that one. Those flights were intelligence work on a mass production basis."

From a British intelligence officer's comments to Allen Dulles on the flights of the U-2 spy planes

War stimulates invention. As a result of World War II, blood plasma and radar were developed, and the effects of the cold war have been no different. Vast government expenditures in science and technology have led to many new discoveries. Some of these have been made by CIA researchers or by researchers financed by the CIA. These inventions frequently involved the secret world of espionage paraphernalia: special listening devices, concealed weapons, and the like. But no CIA-related discovery has been as interesting—or impressive—as the U-2 plane and the equipment designed to go on it.

The U-2 Plane

By 1952, the CIA had come to the conclusion that the intelligence it gathered on the Soviet Union was inadequate. Few Western agents had been able to penetrate Soviet society and operate behind the iron curtain. The number of Soviets working as double agents was very small. The United States had no accurate information on the strength of the Soviet armed forces or on the kinds of new weapons being developed by the Kremlin.

In addition, many in the Agency were dissatisfied with the two principal means of collecting data on the Soviet Union—"humint" and "sigint." Humint was intelligence gathered from human sources; sigint was that gathered from radio and other electronic signals. Both, it was believed, were subject to human errors of judgment, bias, and exaggeration and open to charges of inefficiency and inaccuracy.

President Eisenhower was deeply concerned about this lack of adequate intelligence. In 1953, he appointed a committee to study the possibility of surprise attack from the Soviet Union, and to determine what steps the United States might take to foresee such an attack and prevent it. Eisenhower appointed James Killian, the president of the Massachusetts Institute of Technology, chairman of the committee.

In the fall of 1954, Killian's committee issued a report which recommended that the United States begin reconnaissance flights over Russia and Russia's allies. The committee realized that no plane capable of such flights was now available. But it did know that a design for a high-altitude reconnaissance plane had recently been completed by the chief aircraft designer for the Lockheed Corporation, Clarence "Kelly" Johnson.

Johnson had submitted his design to the Air Force, but the Air Force had turned it down as unworkable. The committee, however, had a different idea. It recommended the plane to the president. President Eisenhower was also impressed with the plan and ordered Allen Dulles to have the plane built by the CIA, as quickly and secretly as possible.

Dulles delegated the authority to one of his top deputies, Richard Bissell, a former economics professor at Yale and MIT. Bissell started to work that very day. He arranged to have the plane financed by the CIA's special appropriations, for which no accounting was necessary. And he telephoned Kelly Johnson and told him to begin construction of the plane.

The plane Johnson and his crew of assistants at Lockheed came up with was called the U-2. It was an extraordinary machine. It could fly as high as 90,000 feet (27,432 m), far above the ceilings of other sophisticated aircraft of the time.

This kept it safe from interception by enemy aircraft and from enemy antiaircraft guns. Moreover, the U-2 could stay aloft for eight to ten hours and cover distances of 4,000 miles (6,437 km) or more, while using a relatively small amount of fuel. Its lightness, its 80-foot (24.4-m) wing span, and its ability to operate at very high altitudes made it a marvel of engineering and technological skill.

The U-2 did have one significant problem. The special fuel— designated as MIL-F-255524A—that had been developed for its engine did not work well at high altitudes. If the plane experienced a flameout at 80- or 90,000 feet (24- or 27,000 m), the pilot had to drop 30- or 40,000 feet (9- or 12,000 m) before he could restart the engine. At these lower altitudes, the plane was vulnerable to enemy attack.

At the same time work had begun on the U-2, work was also begun on the photographic equipment to be carried by the plane. Dr. James Baker, a Harvard astronomer, designed a new camera lens for aerial photography that was superior to anything in use before. From a camera in an airplane 8 miles (12.9 km) high, the lens could read the headlines of a newspaper on the ground. At 13 miles (20.9 km), it could easily distinguish an object the size of a lawn chair or garbage can.

Eastman Kodak came up with a new film which was almost as thin as Saran Wrap. Its thinness made it possible to mount large quantities of the film in a small amount of space. A new camera for the U-2 came from the laboratories of Dr. Edwin Land, the head of the Polaroid Corporation. Known as the B-Camera, it could swing its lens from side to side while snapping pictures in rapid order. These pictures, when placed end on end, formed a composite picture of the area photographed. The camera weighed 450 pounds (204 kg) and was designed to fit into the U-2 fuselage.

The first flight of a U-2 over Soviet territory took place on July 4, 1956. By the second or third flight, the Russians had picked up the plane on their radar, but could do nothing about it because they had no weapon capable of bringing it down. The Soviets referred to the plane as the "dark lady of espionage."

In twelve flights, the U-2 could photograph all the significant information in an area the size of the United States; in thirty flights it could cover the entire Soviet Union. The ultimate goal of the U-2 flights was to photograph every square inch of Soviet territory in order to gain a complete understanding of Soviet military preparations and capabilities. After each U-2 mission, the photographs were analyzed at a special photo-interpretation laboratory that had been set up in Washington, D.C. The amount of information gleaned from the photographs was more than the CIA had ever handled from one source, and it gave the Agency an enormous intelligence-gathering advantage over the Soviet Union.

Testifying before the Senate Foreign Relations Committee after the U-2 flights had been discontinued, Secretary of Defense Thomas S. Gates, Jr., said that the U-2 had "built up a story that gives you a judgment for surprise attacks." And it had also, he added, provided vital information on Soviet "airfields, aircraft, missiles, missile testing and training, special weapons storage, submarine production, atomic production and aircraft deployment."

The U-2 Incident
For almost four years, the U-2 flights continued without any problems. They were rightly regarded as a success for the CIA and American intelligence. But on May 1, 1960, a U-2 crashed within the Soviet Union. The American government badly mishandled the incident, and Soviet leaders turned it into a propaganda broadside against the United States. The U-2 affair created the first major controversy surrounding the CIA.

The problem was timing. A summit conference had been scheduled for May 16, 1960, in Paris. President Eisenhower, Nikita Krushchev of the Soviet Union, and other world leaders were to sit down together and discuss outstanding difficulties in East-West relations. Great hope had been placed on the conference as a means to lessen cold war tensions.

According to Davis Wise and Thomas Ross, authors of *The Invisible Government* (1964), an early indictment of the CIA, Agency officials recognized the risks they took in continuing the U-2 flights as the time for the conference neared. But they nevertheless decided to go ahead with another flight. Many in the Agency feared that the summit conference might result in an agreement between the Soviet Union and the United States that would ban the future use of the U-2, and they wanted to make at least one more intelligence-gathering mission. It should also be noted that President Eisenhower did not order the flights suspended as the conference approached.

Francis Gary Powers, the pilot who was to man the ill-fated flight, was flown from the U.S. base at Incirlik, Turkey, to Peshawar, Pakistan, on April 27. Many U-2 flights originated in Peshawar, from where they flew in a northwesterly direction and landed in Bodo, Norway. Powers was to wait in Peshawar until weather conditions permitted a flight over Russia that would be free of clouds or fog that would obscure photographs taken from a high altitude.

On Sunday, May 1 (a national holiday in the Soviet Union), Powers was ordered to fly his mission. Later, at his trial in Moscow, he testified that he was shown a map of the exact route he was to follow and given a package that contained 7,500 rubles in Russian paper money and several gold coins. There was also a silver dollar which had a "pin" hidden in it. The pin, Powers said, contained poison which he could take if captured.

Powers also knew that his plane was rigged with a destructor unit capable of blowing the U-2 up, so that Soviet experts would not be able to examine its sophisticated construction and instruments. Other equipment on the plane included topographic maps of the Soviet Union and necessities of survival such as fishing gear, a dagger, fire-making aids, food concentrates, flares, a flashlight, compasses, and a revolver with a silencer and 200 rounds of ammunition. He was also given rings and wristwatches that could be used for barter with Russians he might encounter.

As Powers neared Sverdlovsk, a large Russian city in the Ural Mountains about 900 miles (1,450 km) east of Moscow, he radioed that his plane had suffered a flameout and that he had to descend to an altitude of 40,000 feet (12,000 m), where there was sufficient oxygen in the atmosphere to start the engine once again. After that, the bases at Bodo and Peshawar did not hear from him and it was assumed that the U-2 had gone down. No one knew if Powers were alive or if the plane had been demolished in a crash or by its destructive device.

Soviet authorities later claimed that Powers was shot down at 8:53 A.M. by a rocket that caught the U-2 at 68,000 feet (20,700 m). Powers himself testified that he had seen an "orange flash" and then had lost control of his plane. Because of the U-2's rapid descent, he had difficulty at first in bailing out, but finally managed to free himself. His difficulties in bailing out made it impossible for him to activate the plane's self-destruct mechanism without destroying himself in the process. And once free of the plane, he could only hope that the U-2 and its evidence would be destroyed when it crashed.

Powers landed in Russia by parachute, and his plane crashed nearby. Several hours later, when the U-2 failed to land in Norway, news of the missing plane was sent to Washington. At an emergency meeting, top State and Defense Department officials and presidential advisers decided to issue a "cover story" that would disclaim the true purposes of the flight.

The cover story was released to the wire services on May 3. It announced that a single-engine American plane with one man on board was missing near the Soviet border in the mountains of eastern Turkey. The plane, it said, had been one of two sent on a weather reconnaissance mission, but its pilot had radioed that his oxygen equipment was out of order. Efforts were now being made to locate the lost aircraft.

On May 7, Khrushchev told the world that Gary Powers had been captured and that the Soviet Union was in possession of the plane he had flown. In a speech before the Supreme Soviet in the Kremlin, he revealed photographs that had been taken from the U-2. The photographs, he said, proved beyond the shadow of a doubt that the plane was involved in spying and espionage activities. In addition, the Soviet Union had Powers's confession that he was a spy for the United States.

Historians of espionage regard official Washington's behavior in the days following Khrushchev's announcement as inexplicable. In his May 7 speech, Khrushchev had said, "I am prepared to grant that the President had no knowledge of a plane being dispatched to the Soviet Union and failing to return." This offered a means for Eisenhower to excuse the mission and let the affair pass over.

But the opportunity was ignored. Instead, the State Department issued a statement that only exacerbated the situation and angered Khrushchev by placing him in an awkward position. "As a result of the inquiry ordered by the President," the new statement read,

> *it has been established that insofar as the authorities in Washington are concerned, there was no authorization for any flight as decribed by Mr. Khrushchev. Nevertheless, it appears that in endeavoring to obtain information now concealed behind the Iron Curtain, a flight over Soviet territory was probably undertaken by an unarmed civilian U-2 plane.*

The statement amounted to an official admission that the United States was involved in espionage. Other admissions were to follow. On May 11, Eisenhower took responsibility for the U-2 flights and excused them on the basis of national security. The well-being of the United States, he said,

> *must never be placed in jeopardy. The safety of the whole free world demands this. As the Secretary of State pointed out in his recent statement, ever since the beginning of my Administration I have issued directives to gather, in every feasible way, the information required to protect the United States and the free world against surprise attack and to enable them to make effective preparations for defense.*

At CIA headquarters, Allen Dulles was angered by the president's statement. He offered to resign his post as CIA director in order to let the blame fall on him rather than on Eisenhower. His offer was refused. In the Senate, William Fulbright (Democrat, Arkansas) declared that "the President need never have avowed or disavowed" the incident but "should have taken the position of silence in this matter and if anyone had to take responsibility it should have been the head of the intelligence. It shouldn't have been the President, who embodies the whole sovereignty and dignity of the whole American people."

Fulbright maintained that the president, by his admission of the U-2 flights, was claiming the *right* to carry out espionage activities against the Soviet Union, a claim that would inevitably—and unnecessarily—infuriate the Russians. The Russians could understand the *need* for intelligence, but by going public Eisenhower had turned the need into a declaration of right, a "right" that Khrushchev could only meet with a firm denial.

The Russians, Fulbright pointed out, "understand that espionage goes on within certain areas all the time. But they never take full responsibility for it. The head of state does not." Eisenhower's avowal of the flights, he added, had "put Mr. Khrushchev in the position where he could not proceed to treaty with a man who at the same time is asserting the right to violate the sovereignity of his country."

Still further confusion followed. *The New York Times* published a story which said that President Eisenhower had ordered a stop to all U-2 flights over or near the Soviet Union. But the same day the story appeared, James Haggerty, the president's press secretary, declared at a press conference that the president had not stopped the flights. This seemed to imply that the flights would continue, regardless of the controversy brewing over Powers's capture.

The result of the mishandling of the U-2 affair was the collapse of the summit conference and the visit of President Eisenhower to the Soviet Union that was to follow the conference. Not long after the U-2 story had broken, Khrushchev toured Gorki Park in Moscow, where the remains of the plane were on public display. At a news conference in the park, he expressed his anger at what he believed was America's threat to continue the flights and of the U-2 program in general.

"This plane had the President's approval," Khrushchev said. "It's simply unheard of! And after that they expect me to say: 'Oh, what nice fellows you all are!' To do such a thing would mean to have no self-respect." He announced that he was canceling Eisenhower's invitation to the Soviet Union because he could not promise that the Russian people would welcome the American president.

In spite of Khrushchev's mood, Eisenhower decided to go to Paris. From the beginning, the summit conference proved to be a fiasco. Khrushchev used the occasion to denounce the United States and browbeat President Eisenhower. He attacked America for its violation of international law in allowing the U-2 flights over Soviet territory and for the use of countries like Norway and Pakistan for the U-2 takeoffs and landings. One month later, he used his indignation over the flights to break up a ten-nation disarmament conference in Geneva, Switzerland.

Gary Powers went on trial on August 17, 1960—the date of his thirty-first birthday. The U-2 pilot was careful to admit his guilt, and to confess sorrow that his mission had torpedoed the summit conference and had led to an increase in world tension. His defense attorney lambasted the United States for its treacherous activities and pictured his client as a victim of American imperialism. The usual punishment for spies under Soviet law was death, but Powers received a ten-year sentence, largely owing to his willingness to admit guilt. In February, 1962, he was exchanged for Rudolf Abel, a Soviet spy who had been caught in the United States.

Soviet authorities made the most of Powers's trial. It was featured on Soviet TV, and later films of the proceedings were shown throughout the USSR. By September, however, the furor had begun to decline. Khrushchev, in New York to attend a meeting of the United Nations General Assembly, said, "there have always been spies and there always will be spies. We treated Powers leniently."

Critics of the CIA blamed the Agency for the collapse of the summit conference. CIA officials, they said, had been overly zealous in their pursuit of intelligence and had unwisely scheduled a flight close to the Paris conference. Some critics suggested that the CIA had deliberately set out to torpedo the meeting.

For the Agency, however, the attacks were unfair. The U-2 flights had brought American intelligence a wealth of information. The controversy surrounding Powers' capture had been the result of blunders by the president and the State Department. Handled correctly, the incident might have amounted to no more than a slight ripple on the surface of Soviet-American relations. However optimistically the Agency looked upon the affair, there can be no doubt the U-2 incident caused one of the first cracks in the CIA's image. Others would follow.

CHAPTER SIX
THE BAY OF PIGS

*"For some time I have been disturbed by
the way CIA has been diverted from
its original assignment. It has become
an operational arm and at times a
policy-making arm of the Government."*

President Harry S. Truman in 1963

In a syndicated article that appeared in the *Washington Post* on December 22, 1963, former President Truman voiced concerns about the CIA that sound very much like the questions raised in the controversy over the Agency in the 1970s. Truman had been president when the CIA was established in 1947 and had supported its creation. Now he was of a different frame of mind.

"With all the nonsense put out by Communist propaganda . . . in their name-calling assault on the West," he wrote, "the last thing we needed was for the CIA to be seized upon as something akin to a subverting influence in the affairs of other people." Truman had no doubts that America needed an intelligence-gathering organization. But, he added,

> there are some searching questions that need to be answered. I . . . would like to see the CIA restored to its original assignment as the intelligence arm of the President, and whatever else it can properly perform in that special field—and that its operational duties be terminated or properly used elsewhere.

What bothered Truman about many CIA operations was that they appeared to him to violate American traditions. "We have grown up as a nation," he wrote, and are "respected for our free institutions and for our ability to maintain a free and open society." He concluded, however, that "there is something about the way the CIA has been functioning that is casting a shadow over our historic position and I feel that we need to correct it."

Truman had in mind two recent CIA operations—the U-2 Affair and the Bay of Pigs invasion of Cuba in 1961. In the last chapter, we saw how the U-2 Affair upset plans for the Paris summit conference and led to criticism of the CIA. But it was the Bay of Pigs operation that was the Agency's first major calamity and that undermined the CIA's image in the minds of many Americans.

The Background of the Bay of Pigs

On January 1, 1959, the Cuban dictator Fulgencio Batista fled his country for the safety of the Dominican Republic. His government, which was well known for its brutality and corruption, had been overthrown by a band of dedicated guerrilla warriors under the leadership of Fidel Castro Ruz. During the following weeks, Castro took advantage of the political vacuum to establish a new government and on February 16, he was officially declared premier.

The United States at first cautiously accepted the new regime as a welcome relief from the corrupt and unpopular Batista dictatorship. But soon the rapid move of Castro to the left became apparent. The Cuban leader announced his conversion to Marxism-Leninism and declared Cuba's friendship for the Soviet Union. A communist nation had come into being in the Caribbean, only 90 miles (145 km) from the United States.

These events deeply disturbed authorities in Washington as well as many Americans throughout the country. And this concern mounted as it became evident that Castro was relying on the Soviet Union to expand and improve the Cuban armed forces. The military buildup began in 1959. By 1960, secret State Department reports showed that Cuba was receiving 30,000 tons (27,200 m.t.) of arms a year. These included Soviet JS-2 51-ton (46-m.t.) tanks, SU-100 assault guns, T-34 35-ton

(32-m.t.) tanks, 76-mm field guns, 85-mm field guns, and 122-mm field guns.

Technicians and military advisers from Czechoslovakia and the USSR arrived in Cuba along with the weapons to train Cuban troops in their use and deployment. Castro expanded Cuba's ground forces to between an estimated 250,000 to 400,000 troops—which put one out of every thirty Cubans in the armed forces, compared to one out of every sixty Americans in the armed forces of the United States.

Communist Cuba was producing a military establishment ten times larger than Batista's had been, a military establishment that was the largest and best armed in Latin America. To analysts in Washington, this implied two things. One, that the United States might ultimately be threatened if Cuba acquired Soviet missiles and missile launchers. Two, that Castro had plans to export his revolution to other Latin American countries. Both scenarios, of course, were unwelcome to the United States, and the downfall of the Castro government became one of the chief concerns of American policymakers.

CIA efforts against Cuba began in the spring of 1960. At first, the Agency concentrated on propaganda and political warfare, broadcasting anti-Castro and anticommunist information by radio. Contacts were made among the growing American Cuban community, swelled by refugees from Castro's communist regime.

On March 17, 1960, the CIA recommended to President Eisenhower that steps be taken to arm and train Cuban exiles for guerrilla warfare in Cuba. Eisenhower liked the suggestion and gave his approval. Later that year, after the election of John Kennedy to the presidency, the new president-elect was likewise informed of the plans and gave his approval. Historians have noted that the pressures on both men to do something about Castro were enormous and that it would have been difficult for either to refuse.

At CIA headquarters, responsibility for the operation was turned over to Richard Bissell, the same man who had supervised the development of the U-2. The first plan to undergo serious consideration was relatively simple. Twenty-five Cuban exiles would be given guerrilla training by the CIA at the U.S. Army Jungle Warfare School in the Panama Canal

Zone. These twenty-five would then train seventy-five others, and the one hundred would be secretly infiltrated into Cuba, where they would help build a resistance network among anti-Castro Cubans still in Cuba.

But this plan had to be abandoned. It was soon discovered that Castro's police and security forces were stronger than had been estimated. CIA agents sent to Cuba were picked up in a day or two after their arrival. Supplies dropped by airplane rarely reached the anti-Castro groups they had been intended for. In these circumstances, Agency planners came to the conclusion that a traditional guerrilla operation was unfeasible in Cuba and began to develop a more elaborate plan that included an air and sea invasion of the island.

The plan that was finally accepted was a more complex and larger version of the operation seven years earlier in Guatemala. A force of Cuban exiles was to secure a beachhead on Cuba's coastline while a fleet of B-26's was to put Castro's air force out of commission and disrupt transportation and communication lines. Once the beachhead had been secured and a portion of Cuban territory had been "liberated," a group of Cuban exile leaders would be flown to Cuba to form a "provisional government." The United States would then officially recognize the provisional government as the one true government of Cuba.

The spot chosen for the invasion was the Bay of Pigs, on the southern coast of Cuba.* The planners seem not to have envisioned a quick and sudden success for the operation, but they did expect uprisings to take place throughout Cuba in support of the invasion so that Castro would have his hands full restoring order. If need be, the invading force could make its way to the Escambray Mountains, where guerrilla operations could be set up.

At the beginning of the undertaking, the CIA leased or purchased several farms in isolated regions of Florida, where the recruits for the "Cuban Liberation Army" were taken for

---

*In Spanish, "Bay of Pigs" is *Baia de Cochinos*. The Cubans, however, refer to the invasion with the name *Playa Giró*, which is the name of one of the two beaches on the Bay of Pigs where the invading army landed.

training. But to assure greater secrecy and to make it more difficult to trace the operation to the CIA, foreign locations were sought for the training camps. Help came from Guatemala. The Guatemalan president gave his approval for CIA camps to be located in his country, and a Guatemalan millionaire donated land to be used as the CIA saw fit. Before the operation was over, Nicaragua and Honduras had also given support of various kinds, and a radio station that broadcast anti-Castro programs was established on Swan Island off the coast of Central America.

The plans called for an invasion force of between 1,400 and 1,500 men. Most were recruited from Cuban exiles who had been in the upper middle class and who had strongly opposed Castro's revolution. About 250 were students; only about fifty were blacks or mulattoes. In an account published after the invasion by Castro, it was estimated that the invaders and their families had once owned a million acres (.4 million ha) of land, ten thousand houses, seventy factories, ten sugar mills, five mines, and two banks.

Many of the recruits were from the Movement for Revolutionary Recovery (MRR), a moderately right-wing group of Cuban exiles. The MRR was made up of military officers, business and professional men, and former Castro supporters who turned against Castro and fled Cuba when he became communist. The MRR's conservative philosophy appealed to the CIA, but the organization had little support among Cubans still in Cuba. It was primarily a group of disgruntled exiles.

The Agency chose for the most part to ignore the People's Revolutionary Movement (MRP), an exile group that did have important contacts in Cuba and an underground network of anti-Castro Cubans. The MRP was openly leftist. Its leader, "Manolo" Ray, had been a former minister of public works under Castro but had grown disillusioned with the Cuban leader's policies. He had remained in Cuba for eight months after his break with Castro, time enough to build up groups of saboteurs and others willing to work for the overthrow of communism. The MRP's underground network covered all of Cuba and had a seven-man council in each province. The slogan of the MRP was *"Fidelismo sin Fidel"*—"Fidel's reforms without Fidel." But because of their leftist sympathies, MRP members were not welcome in the Cuban Liberation Army.

As leader of the Cuban exile troops, the CIA chose Manuel Artime Buesa. Artime had been a former Castro soldier and had been an official in the Agrarian Reform Zone of Oriente Province. His basic political philosophy, however, was conservative, and he was a devout Catholic. He had little military experience, but his leadership ability was judged to be large.

One of Artime's first moves as leader was to weed out of the Liberation Army anyone he found incompetent or whose loyalties he suspected. He replaced several officers who had been training with the men in Guatemala for several months with officers who had served in Batista's army. Many of the officers from Batista's time were regarded as thugs who had willingly been part of the former dictator's brutal and corrupt regime.

President Kennedy had ordered that the former Batista men, called Batistianos, be excluded from the Liberation Army, but his orders appear to have been disregarded. When 200 of the 1,500 recruits protested Artime's move to place the Batista officers at the head of the Army, the CIA had the protesters isolated from the other 1,300. Most of the 200 were persuaded to return to the Army and accept the Batistianos. But a small number whose loyalty could not be trusted were flown to a jungle prison in northern Guatemala to wait out the invasion.

The large size of the operation violated one of the CIA's most sacred principles: secrecy. From the beginning, the preparations for the invasion were common knowledge in Miami's Cuban community, which was heavily infiltrated by Castro's spies. Furthermore, stories about the invasion were appearing regularly in the American press, written by reporters who had come across bits of information that began to form a pattern.

As early as October 31, 1960—almost six months before it took place—Raúl Roa, the Cuban foreign minister, stated that he had accurate knowledge of the invasion at an interview at the United Nations. Roa named the places the exiles had been trained in Florida and knew of the base in Guatemala. He also knew that the CIA was in charge of the operation. Roa claimed that his information had come from *Life* magazine, the *New York Daily News,* and CBS.

Castro's own intelligence network had picked up accurate and useful information. The Cuban leader used the information to his own advantage. In the days before the invasion, his police and army rounded up men and women suspected of anti-Castro sympathies, perhaps as many as 100,000 altogether, and had at least six of their leaders executed.

Castro also had the Escambray Mountains searched for guerrilla bands, and he also prepared for the invasion by dispersing and camouflaging the small Cuban air force. Possible invasion sites, including the Bay of Pigs, were constantly patrolled and observed. And on the morning of April 15, 1961, the day before the invasion, Castro went to his military headquarters in Havana and ordered a nationwide alert.

The Bay of Pigs Invasion
On April 13, 1961, President Kennedy pledged that the United States would not intervene "under any conditions" to help bring about the downfall of Fidel Castro. He also stated that he would do everything possible "to make sure there are no Americans involved in anti-Castro actions around Cuba" and that he "would be opposed to mounting an offensive" against Castro from this country. One week later, after the failure of the invasion and the discovery of CIA involvement, these words would be embarrassing to the president.

The Liberation Army, divided into six battalions, set sail on April 14 on six ships from Puerto Cabezas, Nicaragua. Nicaraguan dictator Luis Somoza had been on hand to offer encouragement to the men. The next day, the first strike of the Liberation Army's air force was made against Cuba. The strike destroyed at least half of Castro's planes, including B-26's, Sea Furies, and T-33 jet trainers.

On April 16, a Sunday, the members of the provisional government received word in New York that the invasion was about to take place. They went to Philadelphia, from where they were flown to Miami. In Miami they were taken to a house on the outskirts of the city where they were kept in secret, ready to be taken to Cuba if the invasion were successful.

Meanwhile, President Kennedy had approved and then canceled a second scheduled air strike against Cuba, which would have been made in support of the landing of the exile army. The reasons for the cancellation are not completely clear. Perhaps the President believed that the first strike had done sufficient damage to the Cuban air force. Perhaps he was reacting to the protests of UN Ambassador Adlai Stevenson, who had been denying American involvement in the first air strike at the United Nations, while the Cubans were claiming American involvement. In any case, the cancellation of the second strike was considered by many observers to have at least harmed the operation and perhaps doomed it to failure.

At midnight of April 16, the invasion began. The ships anchored a half-mile (.8 km) off the Cuban coast. The first men to land were American frogmen to mark positions. Coral reefs delayed several landing craft and other landing craft experienced engine trouble. One battalion was still at sea and had not landed when dawn came.

The invading force was able to penetrate Cuba a distance of about 20 miles (32 km) without opposition when it encountered Castro's militia. The arrival of heavy reinforcements from other elements of the Cuban army brought about a quick surrender on the part of the exiles.

On that same fateful Monday morning, the remaining planes of Castro's small air force were able to inflict major damage on the invaders. Two ships were sunk, the *Houston* and the *Rio Cándido,* which went down with most of the Liberation Army's ammunition, its oil, communications equipment, and some of its men. Castro's jet trainers, armed with 20-mm cannon—weapons the CIA had not known the Cuban's possessed—shot down three of the invaders' B-26's.

Later that day, Kennedy gave his approval for a second air strike, but the approval came too late. The exile force had been largely defeated. And when the planes finally arrived, they were an hour late because of a misunderstanding over time zones.

After the surrender of the Liberation Army, 1,180 of the 1,297 men who were able to make the landing were rounded up and taken as prisoners to Havana. Many confessed to their CIA connection and spoke of the support they had received from the United States. Castro used the occasion to denounce the United States and to warn other small nations of the dangers of American imperialism and aggressiveness.

When the furor over the invasion died down, American representatives negotiated with Castro for the release of the men of the Liberation Army. Castro requested medical supplies in exchange for the prisoners and, when his request was accepted, released the men in time to go back to Florida for Christmas, 1962. Later Castro claimed that only part of the supplies he had asked for had been delivered and that he had been cheated out of the rest.

Aftermath of the Invasion

The invasion helped to solidify national feeling behind Castro in Cuba—exactly the opposite of what it was intended to do. "The invaders have been annihiliated," Castro declared over the radio on the evening of April 19. "The Revolution has emerged victorious. It destroyed in less than seventy-two hours the army organized during many months by the imperialist Government of the United States."

The invasion and its failure also left a feeling of ill will among the Cuban exiles in Florida. Many blamed President Kennedy for the failure of the operation. In Miami, Manolo Ray denounced what he called the CIA's continued domination of the Cuban resistance movement. He asked that the Agency cease its meddling in Cuban politics and its support for former Batista men.

President Kennedy publicly shouldered responsibility for the operation's failure, but privately he blamed the bad advice he had received from the CIA and from his military advisers. Privately, too, he said that he believed the Agency needed reorganization from top to bottom and a reordering of priorities. Several months later, he accepted Allen Dulles's resignation as CIA director and replaced him with John McCone, a prominent businessman.

The strongest denunciations of the Bay of Pigs operation in the United States came from liberals who felt betrayed by a president they regarded as a liberal. "The President speaks peace," wrote journalist Fred Cook in *The Nation* on June 24, 1961, "but the CIA overthrows regimes, plots internal sabotage and revolution ... directs military invasions, backs right-wing militarists." These actions, he concluded, "are not the actions of a democratic, peace-loving nation devoted to the high ideals we profess." They are the same actions we condemn the communists for taking, except in our case, they are "in right-wing robes."

One of the harshest critiques of the invasion came from within the Agency itself. This report came from Lyman Kirkpatrick, the CIA's inspector general, whose responsibility was similar to that of an ombudsman of Agency activities. Kirkpatrick laid most of the blame for the Bay of Pigs squarely on the CIA. His report was deeply resented by Dulles, Bissell, and others who believed he had betrayed the CIA.

Kirkpatrick noted that the planners of the invasion had made no use of the CIA's Office of National Estimates (ONE). No formal request for expert opinion has been made to that division of the CIA. Indeed, the invasion planners had failed to ask the crucial question: did the CIA's Cuban experts believe that Castro was unpopular enough that unhappy Cubans would support the invading force?

Had the question been asked, the planners would have found that no one in the Office of National Estimates who knew Cuba believed for a minute that Cubans would support the overthrow of Castro. Kirkpatrick did mention that one of the planners had an informal discussion with an ONE staff member shortly before the invasion and was told that the Cuban army would probably remain loyal to Castro in the event of an invasion. But the planner appeared not to have acted on this information and continued to believe the invasion would work.

Other factors Kirkpatrick criticized were the absence of adequate air cover, the problems in maintaining secrecy and security, press leaks, and the political infighting among the exiles, who at times seemed more suspicious of one another than of Castro. But basically what he was condemning was a badly conceived plan, a plan too large to be kept under control, and a plan whose goals were unclear. Had the planners, for instance, really believed that a force of 1,400 men were any match for Castro's army of well over 200,000?

The CIA planners of the Bay of Pigs seemed afflicted with what Denis Brogan, a British scholar, has called "the illusion of American omnipotence." This illusion, that the United States could not fail, led them to believe they could manipulate events in Cuba and bring down Castro. And it led them to believe that Castro could be replaced with a provisional government—selected by the CIA—which could assume control of Cuba and earn the loyalty of the Cuban people.

CIA activity in Cuba did not end with the Bay of Pigs. In 1962, as part of the program of economic warfare against Castro, a shipment of Cuban sugar was contaminated with an ill-tasting, but nonpoisonous substance. Measures such as these were designed to make Cuba's products undesirable and take them off the market.

One reason for the continued CIA interest in Cuba was that President Kennedy and his brother Robert, the attorney general, wanted Castro out. With this in mind, the Agency began to consider a new project, called Operation Mongoose, that would bring down the Cuban leader.

In its planning stages, Operation Mongoose was even more ambitious than the Bay of Pigs invasion had been. It envisioned a triumphal march on Havana to take place in October, 1962, after the liberation of Cuba. Little of the project was carried out, however, except a few raids on the island by small sabotage groups, and the provision of weapons to underground groups.

The most notorious of the Agency's actions against Cuba after 1961 were the several attempts it made on Fidel Castro's life. These assassination plots, each of which failed to take the life of the Cuban leader, will be discussed in Chapter Nine. CIA interest in toppling Castro began to wane in the mid-1960s and died out completely by 1967 and 1968.

More successful was the role played by the Agency in other Cuban-related incidents in the 1960s and 1970s. The first of these was the Cuban missile crisis of October, 1962. The others related to the attempts by Castro and his followers to export the Cuban Revolution to other nations in Latin America.

• The Cuban missile crisis began in the summer of 1962 when thirty Russian ships landed in Cuba. The ships were laden with military equipment and technicians. A concerned President Kennedy called upon the CIA for precise intelligence on Soviet intentions in the Caribbean and approved U-2 aerial photography flights over the island.

By mid-October, through a combination of human and technical intelligence, the Agency was able to offer the president an exact report. CIA informers in Cuba spoke of important new military construction. The Agency's analysts of aerial photographs were able to pinpoint the missile sites under construction and to recognize the types of missiles that could be deployed at the sites.

The Soviet Union claimed that the weapons it sent to Cuba were defensive in nature, but the CIA was able to prove this false. There were short-range missiles that could reach as far as Washington, D.C., and medium-range missiles that could hit almost any city in North America. Armed with this information, President Kennedy challenged the Soviets to dismantle the missile sites. For a few days, war between the United States and the USSR seemed imminent. But the Soviet Union backed down and the missiles were removed. By supplying the president with accurate intelligence, the CIA had played a significant role in a major world crisis—the kind of role it had been created and designed to play.

• Also successful was the CIA's effort to stem the tide of Cuban-inspired revolution in South and Central America. In the years after his victory in Cuba, Castro attempted to bring revolution to most of the nations of Latin America. In the words of Castro's friend and fellow revolutionary, Che Guevara, the purpose was to create "not one but many Vietnams" for the United States to face. American power, Che believed, would not be able to confront leftist revolution in South America on a widespread scale, as well as carry on a major war in Southeast Asia.

To meet this challenge, the CIA kept close track of Cuban activities in Latin America. Advice and support were given to Latin American armies and police forces in the establishment of counterinsurgency and antiterrorist units. The CIA, along with other divisions of the U.S. government, encouraged the governments of Central and South America to resist Cuban-backed revolution and provided assistance when needed. As a result, not one Latin American nation fell victim to a Castro-inspired revolution in the 1960s or 1970s, and Castro's attempts to export the Cuban experience failed. For many in the Agency, the CIA's role in thwarting Castro's plans for Latin America rank among the most important successes in the CIA's history.

But these successes and the impressive role the Agency had played in the Cuban missile crisis did little to clean up the tarnished image the CIA suffered after the Bay of Pigs. Agency loyalists believed that the CIA was forced to shoulder too much of the blame for the failed invasion. After all, two presidents, Eisenhower and Kennedy, had approved the mission and had been sufficiently impressed by the Agency's earlier achievements to give the CIA the go-ahead. Other Americans, however, saw the Cuban disaster as proof that the CIA had too much power and was using this power wrongfully. These people spoke of the need to "tame" the Agency and limit its far-flung activities. The controversy over the CIA had begun, but it was still in its initial stages.

CHAPTER SEVEN

THE CIA IN SOUTHEAST ASIA

*"The temptation to interfere in
another country's internal affairs
can be almost irresistible,
when the means are at hand."*

Victor Marchetti and John D. Marks,
The CIA and the Cult of Intelligence

During the 1960s, the CIA became a symbol of American arrogance for leftists throughout the world. It was denounced as a "hotbed of reactionaries," a "fascist organization," and an "oppressor of foreign peoples." In the United States, leaders of the New Left called for its disbandment. Elsewhere, the mere mention of its initials could evoke extreme disgust and anger.

Much of the anti-CIA feeling was inspired by the role the Agency played in America's involvement in the Vietnam War and Southeast Asia. Much of this feeling, too, was unreasoning, misinformed, and excessive. Nevertheless, it helped to further the collapse of the Agency's reputation and to pave the way for the CIA controversy of the 1970s. That controversy might not have arisen without the massive opposition to the Vietnam War—and to all aspects of government—that preceded it.

The CIA in Laos
The American involvement in Southeast Asia goes back to the late 1940s and early 1950s. The communists had just taken power in China and the countries to the south—Vietnam, Laos, Cambodia, Thailand, and Burma—were considered

vulnerable to communist attack or revolution. Moreover, Japanese occupation during World War II had left these countries in uncertain political and economic circumstances. No one could tell what the future might bring.

Two of these countries were of particular interest to American policy makers and the CIA: Laos and Vietnam. Both were French colonies on the verge of independence and extremely unstable. Both, too, had native communist movements that were supported by China and the Soviet Union.

Laos is a landlocked country about the size of Utah. It received independence from France in 1949, but in the 1950s became increasingly mired in a civil war among three forces: conservatives, communists, who were known as the Pathet Lao, and neutralists, who wanted Laos to be independent of both East and West.

Policy makers in the Eisenhower administration viewed Laos as an important "testing ground" for America's confrontation with communism. John Foster Dulles, the secretary of state and the older brother of CIA Director Allen Dulles, wanted Laos turned into "a bastion of the free world," a showpiece of America's ability to undermine the appeal of communism and establish democracy.

American money began to pour into the country. Most of it was directed toward General Phoumi Nosavan, a right-wing strongman, who was regarded as sufficiently anticommunist. The CIA operation in Laos was one of the largest it ever mounted. It was so extensive that journalist David Halberstam, the author of *The Best and the Brightest* (1972), has written that Laos came "perilously close to being a CIA colony."

The CIA gave General Phoumi advisers to help him learn the techniques of modern warfare. It also arranged for him to have a budget of $3 million a month. But at best Phoumi proved an unreliable ally. He was a cautious general who often shrank from battle, and he was a superstitious man who more often consulted his astrologers than he did his CIA advisers.

In March, 1961, Phoumi's troops turned and ran at a crucial battle with the combined forces of the neutralists and the communists. At the same time, American hopes for a right-wing government collapsed. During the months that followed, Washington—and the CIA—withdrew their support from the general and turned to the neutralists. The millions and millions of dollars that had been spent on Phoumi had been wasted.

But the CIA was to spend many millions more in Laos before the war was over. Agency efforts now concentrated on the creation of an army among a primitive Laotian tribe known as the Meo. The Meo lived in the highlands near the Plane des Jarres. The CIA first began to train them to defend themselves against the Pathet Lao, but the training program soon grew in scope until an army of 30,000 had been formed.

Known as the Armée Clandestine, the Meo troops proved to be one of the most effective fighting forces in Southeast Asia. They wholeheartedly gave of themselves in the struggle against the communists and proved far more reliable than General Phoumi's army had been. But the price paid by the Meo in the war was enormous. Originally a people who numbered about 250,000, only a remnant of about 10,000 escaped into Thailand in 1975 at the time of the final communist conquest of Laos.

Another factor in the CIA's war in Laos was the Agency's private airline, Air America. Air America was wholly owned by the CIA and was used throughout Southeast Asia. In Laos, Air America planes dropped Meo tribesmen of the Armée Clandestine behind communist lines and served many other purposes in the war effort. On at least one occasion, it was used to fly packages of counterfeit Pathet Lao currency into communist-held territory in an attempt to wreck the economy by flooding it with paper money.

In the late 1960s and early 1970s, the CIA financed 4,800 soldiers from the Thai Army who volunteered to serve in Laos. But the additional support was not enough to overcome the final communist thrust that led to a Pathet Lao victory. At the height of the Laotian operation, experts estimate that the United States was spending between $300 million and $500 million per year. But in spite of this enormous expenditure, no program seemed able to bring about a settlement compatible with American interests.

The CIA in Vietman: the First Years

Vietnam is a long, narrow country that stretches for more than a thousand miles (1,600 km) along the South China Sea. It is about the size of New Mexico. In 1884, it became a French colony; in 1940 it was occupied by the Japanese. By that time, a vigorous and popular nationalist movement had sprung up with the goal of freeing Vietnam from both French and Japanese influence. The man who emerged as leader of the nationalists was the communist Ho Chi Minh.

After World War II, Ho and his followers carried on a bloody war against the French, who attempted to reassert their authority in Vietnam. The war lasted from 1946 until 1954, when the Viet Minh, as the communists were known, won a decisive victory over the French at Dien Bien Phu, in northern Vietnam near the Laotian border. The victory, however, did not result in a Vietnam united under Ho. Pressure from the United States and other Western nations caused Vietnam to be divided in half: a North Vietnam under Ho Chi Minh and a South Vietnam under governments sympathetic to the West.

The creation of South Vietnam presented Washington with grave problems. The country had been ravaged by World War II and the war of independence that followed. A variety of groups, warlords, tribes, and other factions vied for power, and there was no single leader with enough prestige and authority to form a strong government. The United States avoided free elections, fearing that Ho Chi Minh, who was popular throughout Vietnam, would win by an estimated 80 percent of the vote.

In 1954, Edward Lansdale, an Air Force colonel who was later to rise to the rank of general, arrived in Saigon (now Ho Chi Minh City), the capital of South Vietnam. He had been sent to Saigon by the American government and with the approval of the CIA to recommend what might be done to establish order and stability. Lansdale had had extensive experience with communist insurgency. During the early 1950s, he had advised Philippine President Ramón Magsaysay on methods to control and destroy guerrilla movement in the Philippines. The guerrillas had been wiped out, and Lansdale had gained an overnight reputation as an expert on unconventional warfare.*

It was hoped that Lansdale could bring similar stability to South Vietnam. During his mission to Saigon, Lansdale became convinced that South Vietnam needed, above all, a strong and popular leader that could unite the country. To Lansdale, the one Vietnamese who could play this role was Ngo Dinh Diem. Diem appeared to have the correct qualifications. He was a strong anticommunist who was at the same time an ardent Vietnamese nationalist. Moreover, he seemed to Lansdale to have genuine leadership ability and to be far superior to anyone else he considered.

On Lansdale's recommendation, Diem became Washington's man in South Vietnam. Elections were held, and Diem polled 98 percent of the vote. In October, 1955, he became South Vietnam's first president. His brother, Ngo Dinh Nhu, became the new government's official political strategist, and his brother's wife, Madame Nhu, emerged as an important figure behind the scenes.

American aid began to flow into South Vietnam at an impressive rate. During the first four years of Diem's presidency, South Vietnam received more than $1 billion from the United States in military and other support. During the same period, the CIA established close relations with the new President and his family.

The major problem faced by the United States and the CIA in South Vietnam was the creation of a nation out of the various peoples and special interests that made up the country. The problem was made more difficult because Washington wanted to create not only a nation, but also a democratic nation, with a political system similar to America's. A free and democratic South Vietnam, it was believed, would be a strong and stable South Vietnam and would contrast vividly with the totalitarian society of North Vietnam.

---

*Lansdale has been the subject of at least two books. In Lederer's and Burdick's *The Ugly American* (1955), he appears as one of the characters, who represents the best type of American abroad. But in Graham Greene's powerful novel *The Quiet American* (1955) he is represented as a naive do-gooder whose plans lead to harm and disruption for the country where he operates.

Before 1959 the communists in South Vietnam, under the National Liberation Front (NLF), had carried out a sporadic guerrilla war. But in 1959, this war expanded and became more fierce. Communist warriors, known as the Viet Cong, carried out a program of terror in the countryside and in major cities. The Viet Cong's tactics were so effective that by 1961, President Diem controlled only one-third of his country. The rest was in the hands of the communists.

To meet the communist threat, the CIA organized, trained, and financed troops called the South Vietnamese Special Forces. Similar to the American troops known as the Green Berets, these crack soldiers were chosen for their courage and military aptitude, and they were expected to provide an effective counterforce to the Viet Cong.

In addition to the Special Forces, the CIA also organized two national police forces, the National Police Field Force, which operated in the countryside and numbered 15,000, and the Special Branch, which worked in the cities and numbered 17,000. A division of the Special Branch was the Saigon secret police, charged with the responsibility of weeding out Viet Cong sympathizers living in the capital city.

In the central highlands of South Vietnam, the Agency supervised the establishment of armies from among the men of two of Vietnam's tribes, the Montagnards and the Nungs. The Montagnards, regarded as subhuman by other Vietnamese, were trained as scouts and border guards. Abandoning their traditional bows, arrows, and spears, they took up modern weapons and proved to be effective fighters. They likewise proved to be an embarassment to the Diem regime, however, because the Montagnard warriors used their new strength to demand for their people autonomy from the Diem regime.

The Nungs were a Chinese people who had fought for the French during the Vietnamese colonial war and then had moved into South Vietnam after 1954. They were known for their fierceness and courage and came to be heavily relied upon by the CIA. They were used to guard CIA installations and to observe and make attacks on communist supply movements and convoys.

But the Nungs, like the Montagnards, brought the Agency special problems. Before they would fight, they demanded a steady supply of beer—no other beverage would do—and prostitutes. CIA officials had to arrange for the transportation of these commodities to Nung locations, at additional cost and bother to the Agency.

The Vietnamese Special Forces, the police units, and the Montagnard and Nung warriors strengthened South Vietnam considerably and helped the Diem regime to gain control of wider sections of the country. But the communist threat continued. In order to undermine the effectiveness of Viet Cong terror in the countryside, American and South Vietnamese authorities initiated a vast program of "relocation."

The relocation program was modeled on the successful "new villages" campaign used by the British against guerrilla bands in Malaya ten years earlier. It sought to move 90 percent of South Vietnam's population into 10,500 strategic hamlets or fortified villages. This operation, it was believed, would make it more difficult for the communists to threaten or control the villages and rural areas. Relocation did improve security, but it also proved disruptive and was resented by many rural South Vietnamese who were forced from their homes to new locations.

The Fall of Diem

Nation building is a difficult and complex process, and while American programs were helping to strengthen South Vietnam in certain areas, in others the Saigon government was losing ground. The Diem regime had never been able to unify the country or to gain widespread popularity.

The problem was the president himself and his family. The aristocratic and closely knit Diems ruled South Vietnam as though it were their personal fiefdom. Moreover, the Diems were devoutly Roman Catholic, a fact that separated them from the vast majority of their fellow countrymen, who are Buddhists.

Nor did the family seriously implement the democratic institutions urged upon South Vietnam by the United States. Diem's government outlawed all opposition parties, leaving the nation only one legal party: his own. And Ngo Dinh Nhu, the president's brother, turned the CIA-trained Special Forces into a police force that enforced loyalty to the Diem family.

In 1960, a group of young army officers attempted to overthrow Diem, but their plot was discovered and suppressed. In 1962, South Vietnamese air force pilots bombed Diem's presidential palace in Saigon. But the most significant and far-reaching protest against Diem and his family developed in 1962 and 1963 and came from Buddhist monks and others in the Buddhist religious community.

The monks disliked the authoritarianism of the Diem government and demonstrated their opposition by self-immolation. On several occasions, monks burned themselves to death after dousing themselves with gasoline and calmly assuming a position of meditation in a prominent city square. The acts were carried by news services throughout the world and presented an ugly picture of life in South Vietnam.

The Diem regime reacted to the protests with contempt. Madame Nhu, the president's sister-in-law, called them "monk barbecue shows." President Diem ordered the Special Forces to attack the Buddhist monasteries in order to disrupt and threaten the monks. These acts of a government headed by a Catholic family only increased dissatisfaction with the regime among the country's Buddhist population.

Early in 1963, American policy makers decided that Diem had to go. The CIA agreed. Diem's failures as president were manifest, and it was obvious that he had become an impediment to the war effort. The Agency had helped bring Diem to power and had lavishly supported him, but it had also maintained contacts with other elements in South Vietnam. Some of these contacts were with a group of dissident generals who wanted to overthrow Diem and establish themselves in power.

The story of the American and CIA involvement in the coup d'état against Diem is told in *The Pentagon Papers*, a collection of secret documents on the Vietnam War published over the protest of the American government in 1971. CIA agents worked closely with the dissident generals, supplying them with intelligence on the Diem government and on Vietnamese troops loyal to the President.

The coup came on November 1, 1963. Diem and his brother were murdered. Madame Nhu fled the country. A new government came into being with the generals at its head. The generals, however, soon fell to bickering among themselves, and their administration proved ineffective. Thereafter, South Vietnam was governed by a succession of military men, none of whom succeeded in unifying the country or in successfully confronting the communist forces.

The CIA in South Vietnam after 1963
After 1965, the American presence in South Vietnam expanded rapidly. By 1968, there were more than five-hundred thousand American troops committed to the war, and the American air force was carrying out regular large-scale bombing missions against North Vietnam. The war had become largely an American affair.

At the same time, the role played by the CIA also increased. CIA stations in South America, Europe, and elsewhere were drained of agents to staff the enlarged Saigon operation, which was maintained under the cover of the Office of Special Assistance (OSA) attached to the American Embassy. More than a thousand agents worked in South Vietnam and ran a variety of programs, ranging from intelligence-gathering to political and covert action missions. In addition, there were at least three thousand contract agents hired by the Agency to carry out special operations.

CIA intelligence-gathering operations in Vietnam met with mixed success. Throughout the war, the communist intelligence network was far superior to that operated by the Agency or the South Vietnamese. Experts believe that the enemy had as many as 40,000 informers in South Vietnam reporting on every aspect of South Vietnam's and America's war effort. These informers gave the Viet Cong a more complete knowledge of American and South Vietnamese activities than the Americans were ever able to acquire of Communist plans and intentions.

Two of the main sources of information about the communists were Viet Cong that had been taken prisoner and captured enemy documents. The CIA set up interrogation centers in each of South Vietnam's forty-four provinces, another in each of the four military districts, and three in Saigon to question the prisoners and examine the documents.

But the problem with these sources of intelligence was that

prisoners could lie and documents could be falsified. Once the communists realized that the CIA relied heavily on documents and captured prisoners, they began to plant misleading information for the Americans to find. Viet Cong agents posing as captured soldiers fed CIA interrogators stories that had been concocted by their superiors.

In addition to the attempt to gather intelligence on the communists in South Vietnam, the CIA also conducted operations across the borders of Cambodia, Laos, and North Vietnam. Small teams of highly trained Vietnamese men were dropped behind enemy lines, where they observed military units and installations and radioed their observations back to the South.

In the case of North Vietnam, these teams frequently carried out sabotage and small-scale raids against the enemy. They were likewise expected to make contact with anticommunist North Vietnamese and attempt to organize underground dissident groups. After 1968, however, the penetration of North Vietnam was brought to a halt because the operation had brought little success. The teams already in place were abandoned. One by one, they were captured by the North Vietnamese, until the last one ceased its radio contact with the South in 1970.

More successful, especially after 1968, was CIA penetration of the South Vietnamese military and political power structure. This was done in order to uncover South Vietnamese officials who secretly worked for the communists and to keep tab on America's South Vietnamese allies. CIA agents kept tab of South Vietnamese police activities, the army, and almost every part of the Saigon government. A CIA wiretap was even placed on the private telephone of the South Vietnamese president.

The Agency put most of its time and energy, however, into the elimination of Viet Cong terrorism. "People's Action Teams" were organized in the nation's 10,500 strategic hamlets. These teams were given training to help them meet the Viet Cong on its own ground and terms, and to protect South Vietnamese villages from repeated communist attack and harassment.

The CIA also established Counter-Terror Teams, of six to

twelve Vietnamese each, whose duty it was to carry the war directly to the enemy. The Counter-Terror Teams penetrated Viet Cong territory, raiding enemy encampments and ambushing convoys. In addition, they would make surprise visits to South Vietnamese villages that had been out of touch with the Saigon government for years. The name Counter-Terror teams, however, quickly proved to be an embarrassment to the South Vietnamese and to the United States and was changed to Provincial Reconnaissance Units (PRU).

One of the most ambitious CIA operations during the Vietnam War was the Phoenix Program. Originally called the Intelligence Coordination and Exploitation Program, the Phoenix Program was a massive and systematic attempt to "neutralize" the "Viet Cong Infrastructure" or VCI. VCI was the way the CIA described the network of communist sympathizers and others, who were forced to support the communists by Viet Cong terror and brutality, on whom the Viet Cong depended in South Vietnam.

Phoenix improved and expanded the antiterrorist units already developed by the CIA. According to William Colby, a CIA official closely identified with the program and who later served as director of the Agency, the purpose of Phoenix was "to capture Communist cadres and bring them in alive so they could be interrogated and exploited for intelligence purposes." The Viet Cong Infrastructure, it was believed, was the primary reason for Viet Cong success, and once its members were identified and isolated, the power of the communists would decline.

The Phoenix Program also met Viet Cong terror and brutality with terror and brutality of its own. In the larger cities, identification of VCI members led to arrest and imprisonment and often to torture and death. In the countryside, it resulted in raids on the areas inhabited by the suspected Viet Cong agents and sympathizers and to summary executions.

In his autobiography, *Honorable Men* (1978), written with Peter Forbath, William Colby estimated that between 1968 and 1971, 28,000 VCI were captured by Phoenix and about 20,000 were killed. South Vietnamese who were part of the program have described occasions when they would enter a man's home at night and shoot him as he slept. As Colby admitted, the word "Phoenix" soon became "a shorthand for all the negative aspects of the war."

Colby maintains, however, that most of the excesses of Phoenix were committed by local Vietnamese officials who used the program to carry out personal political vendettas and to eliminate their own opponents. The program itself, he believes, was successful and by 1975 had eliminated most of the VCI or at least had weakened the VCI considerably.

Colby's assessment is disputed by CIA critics. Wilfred Burchett, a left-wing* Australian journalist who traveled with the Viet Cong for several years and who knew Ho Chi Minh personally, contends that the VCI was still active in 1975 and was used by the communists in their final drive to victory. In the March 1978 edition of *Harper's* he argues that the rapidity of the final communist victory in South Vietnam can only be explained by the help the communists received from the VCI.

CIA attempts to shore up the political and economic life of South Vietnam all ended in failure. No Saigon government would allow the existence of opposing political parties, and the Agency's hopes that a moderate, democratic force would appear to take charge came to nothing. The political base of the government remained narrow and unpopular.

To improve the vitality of the South Vietnamese economy, the CIA tried to interest American corporations in investment in South Vietnam. One by one, however, the corporations refused, pointing to the continued chaos and uncertainty in the country and its uncertain future. When the Agency turned to Japanese businessmen and tried to interest them in investment in South Vietnam, CIA officials were likewise met with refusal.

Throughout the Vietnam War, CIA reports and assessments were consistently gloomy. CIA analysts believed that communist strength and support were large and that the political leaders the United States relied upon in Saigon were weak,

*The intelligence services of Western nations believe Burchett is a communist agent and a paid propagandist.

corrupt, or inadequate. They argued too that the American programs in Vietnam were, for the most part, not working and not achieving the goals they were designed to achieve. These realistic reports, however, were ignored or disregarded by policy makers in Washington, who continued to hope for an American and South Vietnamese victory over the communists.

The final communist drive in South Vietnam took fifty-five days. It was a violent and bloody period, ending in complete disorder and chaos, as thousands of Americans and Vietnamese attempted to leave the country in the last days before the communist take-over. The fall of Saigon has been described in detail by Frank Snepp in *Decent Interval* (1978).

Snepp* was a young CIA agent who served as "resident specialist on government and Communist strategy" in Saigon. He was also in charge of interrogating many of the prisoners captured during the Phoenix Program. One of these prisoners, he writes, was Nguyen Van Tai, believed by the CIA to be the highest-ranking North Vietnamese official ever to be captured.

According to Snepp, one of his superiors in the Agency suggested, just before the communist tanks rolled into Saigon, that it might be "useful" if Tai "disappeared."

> *The South Vietnamese agreed. Tai was loaded on to an airplane and thrown out at ten thousand feet over the South China sea. At that point he had spent over four years in solitary confinement in a snow-white room, without ever having fully admitted who he was.*

Snepp accepts this kind of event as something that can be expected in a long and bitter war. What earned his disgust, however, and caused him to write his book was the sense of betrayal he felt. Snepp believes that the Agency was responsible for the abandonment of thousands of Vietnamese who had worked for the CIA. Moreover, he adds, the CIA made no effort to destroy documents that would be captured by the

---

*Snepp wrote his book without CIA approval, although as an agent he had taken an oath not to divulge his experiences with the Agency without prior consultation with CIA officials. The CIA sued Snepp and won a court settlement that forbade Snepp from receiving any royalties from the book's sales.

communists and which named names of those who had worked for American intelligence.

The communists completed their take-over of South Vietnam at the end of April, 1975. The long war came to an end. For the CIA, which had exerted enormous effort at nation building in Vietnam, it was a difficult defeat and a defeat made more difficult by the controversy over the Agency's activities that was already brewing in the United States. Twenty years earlier, the CIA had gone into Vietnam with optimism and belief that it could contribute to the creation of a democratic and anticommunist nation. When it left Vietnam in 1975, the Agency's morale was the lowest it had been in its twenty-eight year history.

CHAPTER EIGHT

THE CIA ON TRIAL

PART ONE: ILLEGAL DOMESTIC ACTIVITIES

"The greatest dangers to liberty lurk in insidious encroachment by men of zeal, well-meaning but without understanding."

**Supreme Court Associate Justice
Louis Brandeis in 1928**

In the preceding chapters, we have seen how the CIA grew from a small organization created at the beginning of the cold war into a large institution with commitments and activities throughout the world. We saw too how criticism of the Agency appeared at the time of the U-2 Affair and began to snowball after the Bay of Pigs. By 1970, the CIA had become one of the most frequently denounced organizations on earth.

For many Americans no charge made against the CIA was more serious than the allegation that the Agency had carried out illegal activities within the United States. What had the CIA done? What were the nature and degree of its crimes? It was to these questions that the Rockefeller Commission, the panel appointed by President Ford, turned its attention.

The Rockefeller Commission's report to the President was made public on June 10, 1975, after more than five months of investigation. The Central Intelligence Agency, the report said, had engaged in activities that were "plainly unlawful and constituted improper invasions upon the rights of Americans." The report concluded, however, that the "great majority" of the Agency's domestic operations had been lawful and were completely within the restrictions of its charter.

The report systematically listed the charges that had been brought against the CIA, described the evidence of CIA wrongdoing, and gave recommendations for change that might prevent similar occurrences in the future. It also made new disclosures about illegal activities that had been discovered in the course of the Commission's investigation.

The two congressional committees also contributed to the investigation of the Agency's domestic activities. The report issued by the Senate Select Committee mentioned facts and incidents not covered in the Rockefeller report and made additional suggestions for reform. The Select Committee from the House of Representatives looked into the efficiency and accuracy of CIA reporting and analysis of international crises. But it was the Rockefeller Commission that made the primary contribution to the nation's understanding of the CIA's domestic operations.

CIA Opening of Private Mail

The Rockefeller Commission confirmed that the CIA conducted a campaign to open the mail of private citizens. The program began in 1952, at the height of the cold war, and concentrated on mail to and from the Soviet Union that passed through the main New York City post office. The purpose of the program was to identify persons working for Soviet intelligence and to investigate the techniques of Soviet mail censorship.

The Agency informed the postmaster general of the United States and the attorney general and received their approval. But it was not clear, the Commission said, if these authorities were given a clear idea of the extent of the CIA project. At first, only the covers of the envelopes were examined, but in 1953, the Agency began to open the mail.

The Rockefeller panel found a CIA memorandum dated 1962 which showed that the Agency was aware that it had violated federal law which prohibited the "obstruction" or "delay" of the mails. But the program had been allowed to continue until 1973, when it was terminated because the Chief Postal Inspector "refused to allow its continuation without an up-to-date high-level approval."

During the last year of the program, 1972, the CIA examined 2,300,000 "items" out of the 4,350,000 items that went through the New York Post Office to and from the USSR. It photographed the covers of 33,000 envelopes and opened 8,700. The New York program was the largest mail intercept operation run by the Agency. But similar operations were run for short periods in San Francisco between 1969 and 1971, in Hawaii in 1954 and 1955, and in New Orleans in 1957.

"While in operation," the Commission report concluded, "the CIA's domestic mail opening programs were unlawful." Specifically, it charged that the openings raised "Constitutional questions under Fourth Amendment guarantees against unreasonable search" and posed "possible difficulties with the First Amendment rights of speech and press."

The Senate Select Committee disclosed other facts about the CIA mail-intercept program. CIA men at the New York Post Office had worked from a "watch list" of at least 1,300 persons who were targeted for surveillance by the Agency. But the agents frequently strayed from their list and looked into the mail of prominent U.S. citizens—mail that had nothing to do with the Soviet Union.

The mail of Richard Nixon and Senators Edward Kennedy and Hubert Humphrey (Democrat, Minnesota) had been opened and copied. Frank Church, the Chairman of the Senate committee, noted that he had discovered a letter he had written to his mother-in-law in the CIA files. Other prominent Americans whose mail had been copied were civil rights leader Martin Luther King, Jr., and his wife, Coretta King, John D. Rockefeller IV, president of Chase Manhattan Bank, Arthur Burns, chairman of the Federal Reserve Board, and Representative Bella Abzug (Democrat, New York). The mail of the Rockefeller Foundation, the Ford Foundation, and Harvard University had also been opened and copied.

Special Operations Group—
"Operation CHAOS"

Another significant section of the Rockefeller Commission's report dealt with the CIA's Special Operations Group. The Special Operations Group had been established in 1967 at the order of President Johnson. It was charged with the responsibility to "collect, coordinate, evaluate, and report on the extent of foreign influence on domestic dissidence."

The creation of the Group reflected President Johnson's belief that anti-Vietnam War sentiment and racial unrest in the United States were being manipulated and financially supported by enemies who wanted to undermine American society. The 1960s and early 1970s, the Commission noted,

were marked by widespread violence and civil disorders. Demonstrations, marches and protest assemblies were frequent in a number of cities. Many universities and college campuses became places of disruption and unrest. Government facilities were picketed and sometimes invaded. Threats of bombing and bombing incidents occurred frequently. In Washington and other major cities, special security measures had to be instituted to control the access to public buildings.

It was this unrest the Special Operations Group was to investigate.

The Special Operations Group, or Operation CHAOS as it was also called, began in August, 1967, and continued for more than six years. Its staff was repeatedly increased to meet renewed presidential demands for information, first under Johnson and then under President Nixon. At its largest, in 1971, the staff numbered fifty-two CIA employees. The activities of Operation CHAOS rapidly declined by the middle of 1972 but were not terminated until March, 1974.

The operation CHAOS staff compiled more than 13,000 different files, which included 7,200 files on American citizens. The files contained the names of more than 300,000 persons and organizations, which were entered into the CIA's computerized index for easy retrieval. With this information, the Special Operations Group wrote 3,500 memoranda for use within the CIA. It turned a large number of these memoranda over to the FBI and sent thirty-seven memoranda for use by the White House and other top-level officials.

In late 1969, Operation CHAOS sent agents overseas to investigate possible foreign connections of American dissidents. At this time, several American dissidents were recruited to serve as informers on their organizations and a number of CIA personnel were ordered to join dissident groups in the United States and report on their activities.

The Rockefeller Commission found that "most of the Operation's recruits were not directed to collect information domestically on American dissidents." But "on a number of occasions," such information was reported by the undercover agents and kept in CIA files. On three occasions, however, an agent of Operation CHAOS was specifically ordered "to collect domestic intelligence."

There was no evidence, the Commission's report concluded, that Operation CHAOS used electronic surveillance, wiretaps, or break-ins in the United States to obtain the information it sought. But there was no question that the Operation "unlawfully exceeded the CIA's statutory authority." Much of the "large quantities" of information that was collected did not relate to the question of foreign connections of American dissidents, and was therefore clearly beyond the scope of the CIA's responsibilities. Moreover, it was "improper" for the Agency to deal with purely domestic matters, as it did in a portion of one major study prepared by the Operation.

One of the Special Operations Group's chief problems, the Rockefeller Commission concluded, was its "excessive isolation" within the CIA. This made it difficult for any meaningful review of its activities to be carried out, including a review by the Agency's Counterintelligence Staff, of which Operation CHAOS was a part. This isolation also made it possible for "the Operation to stray over the bounds of the Agency's authority without the knowledge of senior officials."

In addition to the 7,200 files on American citizens collected by Operation CHAOS, the CIA kept other files and indices. Altogether, the CIA's Directorate of Operations has indexed over 7,000,000 names of people of all nationalities. About 115,000 of these were names of Americans.

Files of detailed information were kept on individuals the Agency "believed to be of possibly continuing intelligence interest." Among these, 57,000 out of a total of 750,000 were on American citizens. The Rockefeller Commission believed that most of the indexed names and the detailed files were "necessary and proper" to CIA business. It added, however, that the Agency at some points in its history had accumulated materials "not needed for legitimate intelligence or security purposes" and in these cases, the files were illegal and improper.

Wiretaps, Buggings, Break-ins,
and
other Questionable Acts

The Rockefeller panel found that the CIA's Office of Security from time to time used methods which were questionable and which intruded on the privacy of individuals. They included physical and electronic surveillance, unauthorized entry, mail covers and intercepts, and reviews of individual federal tax returns. These methods had been used to uncover the sources of leaks of classified and secret Agency information to the public.

The Commission found that "the large majority" of the Office of Security's work concerned persons affiliated with the CIA: "employees, former employees, and defectors and other foreign nationals used by the Agency as intelligence sources." In these cases, the Office of Security's investigative methods were completely within the CIA's authority.

The Commission maintained that there was no evidence that illegal investigations had been "directed against any congressman, judge, or any other public official," as had frequently been charged in the press. But it did find fourteen instances in which the Office of Security had exceeded its authority. Five of these investigations were directed against newsmen, in order to discover their sources of information. Nine others were directed against private citizens in other fields of endeavor.

The Commission report summarized the Office of Security's violations as follows:

• The Office had used wiretaps on thirty-two occasions, the last in 1965. It has used bugs in thirty-two instances, the last in 1968. And it had carried out twelve break-ins, the last in 1971. "None of these activities," the report pointed out, "was concluded under a judicial warrant, and only one with the written approval of the Attorney General."

• On sixteen occasions, the Office of Security acquired information from the Internal Revenue Service on the personal income tax records of individuals to determine if they were security risks or had connections with foreign groups. In each case, the CIA did "not employ the existing statutory and regulatory procedures for obtaining such records."

• In ninety-two instances, the Office of Security photographed the fronts and backs of mail belonging to individuals under investigation. In twelve cases, "letters were intercepted and opened." All of these activities violated existing laws governing the flow of mail.

• In an unspecified number of instances, the Office of Security carried out physical surveillance against private citizens. The last such instance was in 1973. Such surveillance is legal unless it reaches the point of harassment, but the Commission's report gave no indication if these cases had remained within legal bounds or had violated individual rights.

In its investigation of these activities, the Rockefeller panel admitted that its information could be inaccurate. "The state of the CIA records on" wiretaps, break-ins, and other questionable operations, the report said,

is such that it is often difficult to determine why the investigation occurred in the first place, who authorized the special coverage, and what the results were. Although there was testimony that these activities were frequently known to the Director of Central Intelligence and sometimes to the Attorney General, the files often are insufficient to confirm such information.

CIA Involvement in Improper
White House Activities
The break-in at the Democratic National Headquarters at the Watergate Hotel occurred in July, 1972. Subsequent inves-

tigation showed that each of the burglars caught in the Watergate and one of their superiors, E. Howard Hunt, had connections with the CIA. Some were former employees, others were still on small retainers from the Agency.

Had the CIA been involved in the Watergate Affair? That was one question that had to be settled. But there were others. As the Watergate scandal unfolded, it was alleged that the CIA was involved in other instances of White House wrongdoing, even before the break-in at the Watergate. Had the Agency carried out illegal activities at the orders of the President?

The Rockefeller Commission found evidence to support the following cases of CIA and White House cooperation in questionable or improper operations:

• In 1971, the CIA provided E. Howard Hunt with equipment and materials. These included a tape recorder, camera, film and film processing equipment, alias documents, and disguises that altered physical appearance and the voice. The requests for these materials had come from members of the White House staff. Hunt used the materials to carry out some of the illegal activities revealed in the Watergate Affair.

• In 1971 and at the request of the White House staff, the CIA did a personality profile on Daniel Ellsberg. Ellsberg was the former Defense Department employee who had turned "The Pentagon Papers" over to the press. Psychiatric experts in the Agency had long been in the practice of drawing up character sketches of foreign leaders in order to assess their strengths and weaknesses. The White House evidently wanted the personality profile to help in a program that was being carried out to discredit Ellsberg.

• Sometime during his first administration, President Nixon and his staff insisted that the CIA turn over "highly classified files" on the Bay of Pigs, the Cuban Missile Crisis, the Vietnam War, and other significant crises to the White House. The files, the President claimed, were needed in the performance of his duties, but they were actually to be used in a campaign against his political enemies.

• During the Watergate investigations, the CIA received requests for information and assistance. The Agency responded to these requests on occasion with incomplete information or delayed delivery of the information. It also destroyed materials that may or may not have been relevant to the investigations.

In the first three instances mentioned above, the Rockefeller panel found that the CIA had been remiss in its responsibilities. Even though the requests had come from the White House, the Agency should have exercised better judgment before supplying the materials and information requested.

In the fourth case, the panel believed that the CIA had behaved poorly and failed to live up to its obligations to provide information to properly designated authorities. But it concluded that there was "no evidence that the CIA participated in the Watergate break-in or in the post-Watergate cover-up by the White House." What the evidence did show, on the other hand, was "a pattern for actual and attempted misuse of the CIA by the Nixon administration." Rather than having been an active participant in the events surrounding Watergate, the Agency had been exploited and victimized by a White House that exceeded its authority and abused its power.

The CIA Handling
of Defectors
From time to time, the CIA takes responsibility for the debriefing of defectors from the Soviet Union and other communist nations. These defectors are often high-level communist officials who may have valuable information that can be used by the Agency. The CIA is always suspicious, however, that defectors may be Soviet agents sent to the United States in order to gain acceptance in America, penetrate American intelligence, and later begin work as a double agent, turning information over to the USSR.

The Rockefeller Commission found that in one case, the CIA held a defector for three years, far longer than any other defector had been held. Moreover, he had been forced to exist "in solitary confinement under spartan living conditions." The reason for the long confinement had been the inability of CIA officials to decide whether his defection had been genuine or if he were a double agent.

The Commission likewise found that on another occasion, a defector had been physically abused by the CIA agent questioning him. In this case, the agent had been fired when the Agency discovered the abuse. But the Commission concluded that the CIA had acted unlawfully in both cases and stated that such treatment should never occur again.

The CIA and Drugs

The Rockefeller panel looked into allegations that the CIA experimented with mind-altering drugs. It learned that the Agency's Directorate of Science and Technology had worked with LSD and other chemicals "as part of a program to test the influence of drugs on humans."

LSD had been given to several persons, all CIA personnel, who were unaware that they were being tested. On one occasion, in 1953, one individual died, apparently from the effects of taking the LSD. Ten years later, in 1963, the CIA's Inspector General had discovered the existence of the drug experimentation program, and the Agency instituted strict new procedures that prohibited the testing of drugs on unsuspecting subjects. In 1967, all drug-testing programs in the CIA were discontinued.

The Commission concluded that the testing of drugs on the unsuspecting was "clearly illegal" and expressed relief that the program had been discontinued. Drug testing had been initiated by the CIA during the early years of the cold war to see if chemicals could be found that could manipulate and control human behavior. John Marks, in his book, *The Search for the Manchurian Candidate* (1979)*, has given a detailed description of the origins and development of the program.

The Manchurian Candidate was the title of a popular suspense novel and movie. It told of an American soldier who was captured by the communists during the Korean War, "brainwashed," and trained to kill on command without knowing what he was doing. The soldier was then released and returned to the United States, where he was to be used to assassinate a prominent politician when the right time came.

Questions about the use of drugs first arose when CIA analysts noticed that Americans and other Westerners captured by communists often lost their commitment to democracy and began to believe in the "rightness" of communism. They seemed to be "brainwashed." Their former personalities had dissolved and a new personality had been constructed. Had these changes been brought about by the communists through the use of special drugs?

The CIA program hoped to discover these drugs and explore the possibility of mind control. The program, however, ended in failure. No drug could be found that rendered human behavior completely manageable to outward suggestion. More often than not, the drugs resulted in behavior that was neither predictable nor controllable. This was the case with Frank R. Olsen, the CIA employee who died after taking LSD.

Olsen was a CIA researcher who worked on methods of biological warfare. Two weeks before his death, he took LSD as part of the Agency's drug-testing program. His wife claims that he had no knowledge that he was taking the drug at the time he took it.

The LSD changed Olsen's personality completely. He became melancholic and morose, and talked of leaving his job with the Agency. His mental state became so poor that he was taken to New York, at CIA expense, to consult with a psychiatrist. It was there that he committed suicide by jumping from a tenth story window of the Statler Hilton Hotel in Manhattan. More then twenty years later, after Olsen's story had broken in the press, President Ford issued a public apology for the tragedy to Olsen's family.

The CIA and Deadly Toxins
The CIA development and storage of deadly toxins—chemicals produced by living organisms—was revealed by the Senate Select Committee. The story was made public on September 9, 1975, when Senator Church announced that his committee had learned of the existence of a cache of deadly chemicals and biological weapons at a secret CIA installation. The cache included a shellfish toxin, Cobra venom, strychnine,

cyanide pills, and a substance known as BZ which attacks the central nervous system.

The cache contained only eleven grams of the shellfish toxin and eight grams of the Cobra venom, but both were extremely potent. The eleven grams of shellfish toxin, according to Senator Church, were enough to kill "hundreds of thousands" of people if administered with "sophisticated equipment." The two poisons had been manufactured in a project known as MKNAOMI or M.K. Naomi which the CIA had carried out in collaboration with the Army.

MKNAOMI developed a variety of weapons, including bullets containing poison darts, spray canisters, and spray pens that could be used against individuals or against small groups. But it likewise did experimentation and research into large-scale covert use of biological weapons.

The report issued by the Senate Select Committee admitted that the original purpose of MKNAOMI was "difficult to determine."

Few written records were prepared during its 18-year existence; most of the documents relating to it have been destroyed; and persons with knowledge of its early years have either died or have been unable to recall much about their association with the project.

"However," the report concluded, "it is fair to conclude from the types of weapons developed for the CIA, and from the extreme security associated with MKNAOMI, that the possibility of first use of biological weapons by the CIA was contemplated."

The problem with this was that "first use" of biological weapons was against a long established American policy. The United States had renounced first use of such weapons in 1925 and again in 1943. President Nixon renewed this policy on November 25, 1969, when he stated that America would not use any form of biological weapon that killed or incapacitated its victims.

Two and a half months later, Nixon further clarified his statement by issuing an executive order banning the use of toxins as weapons by the United States. The executive order instructed that all American stockpiles of toxins be destroyed. Contrary to the President's wishes, however, a CIA scientist acquired the supply of shellfish toxin and the cobra venom and stored them at a CIA laboratory.

The Select Committee could not decide if this had been a willful violation of presidential order. It may well have been the result of excessive secrecy. The mid-level CIA employee who stored the toxins did not make a record of his act, for the sake of secrecy, and the high-level officials responsible for carrying out the President's order rarely wrote down their directives to mid-level personnel, once again, for the sake of secrecy. The illegal storage of the toxins may therefore have been the result of a failure of communication.

The Recommendations

The Rockefeller Commission listed thirty recommendations for reform of the CIA. The recommendations were directed against the abuses the Commission had uncovered, and they fell into three general areas. The Senate Committee recommendations paralleled the Rockefeller recommendations, and can be divided into the same three areas.

First, the Rockefeller Commission believed that there should be a more precise definition of what the CIA should and should not do. There should be a written code of proper conduct for officials and agents. The Commission advised that the National Security Act of 1947 be amended to "make explicit that the CIA's activities must be related to foreign intelligence," not domestic. It also suggested that "the Agency should issue detailed guidelines for its employees further specifying those activities within the United States which are permitted and those which are prohibited...."

The Rockefeller panel was especially harsh on a secret arrangement that had been made in the 1950s between the Justice Department and the CIA. This agreement had enabled the Agency to decide for itself whether CIA employees involved in alleged criminal misconduct should be prosecuted, and thus had given the Agency law-enforcement powers which it could not legally possess. The agreement had also represented an abdication by the Justice Department of its constitutional authority, the panel believed, and should be brought to an end.

The second category of recommendations issued by the Rockefeller Commission stressed the importance of CIA internal reform and reorganization. These recommendations called for "increased lateral movement of personnel among the directorates" of the Agency and for efforts "to bring persons with outside experience into the Agency at all levels." The CIA would thereby experience a turnover of new ideas and new blood.

The Commission believed that an important step in reorganization would be the upgrading of the office of CIA Inspector General, which reviews Agency activities and judges if they are efficient and acceptable. It recommended that the Inspector General's authority to patrol the Agency be broadened, especially in domestic matters.

The third group of recommendations offered suggestions for increased oversight of the CIA by congressional and executive committees. Congress, the Commission pointed out, "should give careful consideration to the question whether the budget of the CIA should not, at least to some extent, be made public...." Control of the budget, after all, had been granted Congress by the Constitution and was therefore one means that Congress had to control the CIA.

The Commission also recommended that Congress set up a Joint Committee on Intelligence to assume the same oversight role over the CIA that the Armed Services Committee had over the military. And it recommended that the President expand the functions of his Foreign Intelligence Advisory Board to include oversight of the CIA.

This expanded oversight board should be composed of distinguished citizens with varying backgrounds and experience. It should be headed by a full-time chairman and should have full-time staff appropriate to its role.

The Board should have "access to all information on the CIA" and should be "authorized to audit and investigate CIA expenditures and activities on its own initiative." A congressional oversight committee and a presidential committee with expanded powers, the Rockefeller panel believed, would go a long way toward checking the excesses the CIA might commit in the future.

Public reaction to the Rockefeller Commission report was generally favorable. The sober and dispassionate descriptions of CIA abuses followed by recommendations for change struck most observers as a valuable contribution toward a solution of the whole CIA controversy. The Commission condemned the CIA for its excesses, but had made carefully designed recommendations that would not weaken America's intelligence-gathering capability.

"So far from being a 'whitewash,'" the *Washington Post* editorialized, "the Rockefeller Commission report is a clear summons to professionalism in intelligence and to respect for Americans' rights." *The New York Times* agreed. "Although the revelations are disturbing," a *Times* editorialist wrote,

> *the fact that they are aired is reassuring and uniquely American. Other nations, even those that are free and self-governing, do not open wide so many closet doors of their foreign intelligence services. These controversies and investigations are a testament to the inherent vigor of this nation's freedom.*

Other writers pointed out that the illegal activities carried out by the CIA were regrettable and were clear violations of American traditions. But these activities, they added, fell far short of the activities carried out by secret police forces in totalitarian societies, where government surveillance of the lives of private citizens was commonplace.

The House Select Committee
on Intelligence

Of the three committees that looked into the activities of the CIA in the mid-1970s, the House Select Committee on Intelligence contributed the least. From the beginning, the House investigation was marked by disputes and quarrels among the committee members. At one point, the original committee was disbanded and then re-formed with a new committee chairman and an enlarged membership.

The new committee, under Otis Pike (Democrat, New York), set to work, but its effectiveness had been permanently marred by the disputes surrounding the earlier committee. Hearings were held and testimony was taken, but the proceedings were largely ignored by the press and public. Nevertheless, in spite of the difficulties facing the committee, some interesting facts did emerge that bore on the problems facing the CIA.

These facts dealt with the efficiency of the CIA and its effectiveness as an intelligence-gathering organization that could predict crises before they arose—areas totally ignored by the Rockefeller Commission and the Senate Select Committee. The House committee found that:

• Analysts at CIA headquarters had failed to predict the 1973 Arab-Israeli War. Only hours before the Arab attack on Israel, the Agency had issued a report that stated "we can find no hard evidence of a major, coordinated Egyptian-Syrian offensive."

• The 1974 coup d'état that toppled the conservative government of Portugal and threw Portugal and its African colonies into turmoil had come as a complete surprise to the Agency. No one had forecast it, and no one seemed prepared to deal with its consequences.

These revelations led Chairman Pike to wonder if the CIA could be trusted to do its job. At a September 28, 1975, appearance on CBS's "Face the Nation," he said that "if an attack were to be launched on America in the very near future, it is my belief that America would not know that the attack was about to be launched." The problem, he added, "was not the amount of information" the CIA was getting, but the Agency's "inability to absorb it." "Above the gathering level ... it just bogs down every single time. It is not absorbed, it is not delivered."

Coming at any other time, these attacks on the CIA's functions might have had more telling effect. They did, after all, question whether the Agency was fulfilling—indeed if it could fulfill—its basic responsibilities. The more spectacular revelations, and the better prepared and far superior reports of the Rockefeller Commission and Church Committee, however, dominated the news and gained most people's attention. Questions about the CIA's efficiency died down until they were revived in recent years by those concerned with the Soviet Union's military expansion and the increased role Russia seemed to be playing throughout the world.

CHAPTER NINE

THE CIA ON TRIAL

PART TWO: PROBLEMS ABROAD

"The United States must not adopt the tactics of the enemy. Means are as important as ends. Crisis makes it tempting to ignore the wise restraints that make men free. But each time we do so, each time the means we use are wrong, our inner strength, the strength which makes us free, is lessened."

From the epilogue of the Senate Select Committee's *Interim Report* on CIA involvement in the assassinations of foreign leaders.

Critics of the CIA have long questioned the Agency's covert involvement in foreign nations. The United States, their argument runs, does not have the right to enforce its own will and self-interest abroad. Such activity usually courts disaster, arouses hatred for America, and never accomplishes the tasks it sets out to accomplish.

These criticisms were at the heart of the Senate Select Committee's report on CIA activities. The Committee looked at two forms of covert action the Agency had allegedly carried out: assassination plots against foreign leaders and a systematic attempt to undermine and overthrow a duly elected President of Chile. In both cases, it found that the CIA had been responsible for acts that were regrettable and that violated the best American traditions.

The Assassination Plots

One of the gravest charges against the CIA was that it had been responsible for the murders of several foreign leaders. The Rockefeller Commission had studied these charges, but its report on assassinations was withheld by President Ford, pending further investigation. The subject was likewise taken up by the Senate Select Committee, also known as the Church

Committee, after its chairman, Senator Frank Church. The Committee issued its report on November 20, 1975.

The Church Committee's investigation had been thorough. Over 8,000 pages of testimony from seventy-five witnesses had been compiled. In addition, the committee had examined documents and files in the presidential libraries of Dwight Eisenhower, John Kennedy, and Lyndon Johnson. The evidence was compressed into 350 pages, in which the five cases of CIA involvement in assassination plots were closely examined: Patrice Lumumba of the Congo (now Zaire), Fidel Castro of Cuba, Raphael Trujillo of the Dominican Republic, Ngo Dinh Diem of South Vietnam, and General René Schneider of Chile.

In three of the assassinations—Trujillo, Diem, and Schneider—the senators found no trace of direct involvement by the CIA. The cases of Lumumba and Castro, however, were different. The committee concluded that "officials of the United States government initiated and participated" in plots directed against the Congolese and Cuban leaders, but had failed in both cases.

Castro was still alive and the poisons that the CIA had earmarked for use against Lumumba were never used. Lumumba had been killed before the CIA assassins could reach him. The committee could say, therefore, that "no foreign leaders were killed as a result of assassination plots initiated by officials of the United States."

The Case of Patrice Lumumba. Patrice Lumumba was a Congolese political leader regarded by his admirers as a national hero and by his enemies as extremely dangerous and unpredictable. But no one can deny his political talents. In 1958, he founded the Mouvement National Congolais (MNC), which sought to gain independence for the Congo from Belgium. He had many loyal, even fanatical followers and was known for his ability to sway crowds by the brilliance of his oratory.

On June 30, 1960, Congolese independence was declared. Lumumba became his country's first premier and Joseph Kasavubu its first president. Within two weeks, however, civil war had broken out. A UN peacekeeping force was sent to help restore order, but Lumumba and Kasavubu announced that they were considering a request to the Soviet Union for aid.

The disturbances in the Congo troubled the United States because the Congo supplies two-thirds of the world's cobalt and is also rich in cadmium, zinc, copper, and other important minerals. A turn toward Moscow by the new Congolese leadership was unthinkable, and at the end of July, Lumumba, on a trip to Washington, received a pledge of American aid from the secretary of state.

Lumumba, however, was regarded with deep suspicion by American officials. There was evidence that he not only welcomed support from the Soviet bloc, but had also received aid and advice from Soviet agents in the Congo. At meetings of the National Security Council in the middle of August, it was decided that Lumumba had to be retired. CIA Director Allen Dulles cabled the Agency's Congo station that Lumumba's "removal must be an urgent and prime objective...."

On September 14, Joseph Mobutu, the chief of staff of the Congolese army, seized political power in a coup d'état. Lumumba fled and sought the protection of a contingent of the UN police force. But the CIA still regarded him as a threat and the plans for his "removal" continued.

CIA officials found a likely assassin and gave him the code name WI/ROGUE. A report from the Agency's Africa Division gave the assassin's qualifications:

He is indeed aware of the precepts of right and wrong, but if he is given an assignment which may be morally wrong in the eyes of the world, but necessary because his case officer ordered him to carry it out, then it is right, and he will dutifully undertake appropriate action for its execution without pangs of conscience. In a word, he can rationalize all actions.

In late September, 1960, poisons to be used to assassinate Lumumba were delivered to the Congo by a CIA agent, but in the disorder of the civil war, they were never used. On December 1, Lumumba was captured by forces loyal to Mobutu and imprisoned at Thysville. On January 17, 1961, he was transferred to Elizabethville by Congolese government authorities and murdered by officials of the local province.

There was no evidence, the committee report concluded, that tied the CIA in any way with the Congolese officials who assassinated Lumumba.

The Case of Fidel Castro. The Church Committee found that "the effort to assassinate Castro began in 1960 and continued until 1965." During this period, the Agency considered a variety of methods to murder the Cuban leader. Some of these were bizarre. There were, for instance, plans to take advantage of Castro's fondness for cigars and scuba diving by arranging to have him supplied with poisoned cigars or a diving suit contaminated with toxins. Another idea had him killed by an "exploding seashell" that went off near where he swam. These plans never got beyond the laboratory stage.

Other plans, however, were carried far beyond the stage of initial preparation. In August, 1960, CIA officials first discussed the possibility of using underworld figures to eliminate Castro. Organized crime, the Mafia, had been active in Cuba before Castro and had contacts on the island that could be exploited. Moreover, assassination and murder were part of the everyday world of the Mafia. Someone involved in organized crime would have no difficulty finding a paid assassin, or "hit man," to perform the deed.

To help set up Castro's assassination, the CIA approached Robert Maheu, a former FBI agent who was later to direct Howard Hughes's businesses in Nevada. Maheu arranged for John Roselli, an underworld figure, to work with the Agency. Two CIA operatives were assigned to accompany Roselli to Miami and assist him in putting together an assassination team.

The first unsuccessful attempt on Castro's life was made in March or early April, 1961. Over the next two years, five more assassination teams were sent against the Cuban leader. On at least two occasions, Roselli made trips to Miami to deliver poison pills to the teams. The attempts failed because no one was found who could be trusted to administer the poison to Castro's food or drink. The last attempt on Castro's life by organized crime was made in late February or early March, 1963.

The failure of the criminal world to assassinate Castro did

not deter the CIA's plans for assassination. In late 1963, a CIA agent known as AM/LASH was given a poison pen device to be used against Castro, and in early 1965, AM/LASH was put in contact with the leader of an anti-Castro group and given a weapon with a silencer. These plans too came to nothing.

The Case of Rafael Trujillo. The case of Trujillo provides an example of a CIA operation against a right-wing dictator. Trujillo had governed the Dominican Republic since 1930. His dictatorship was brutal and an embarrassment to the United States. By the late 1950s, Washington had come to the conclusion that the Trujillo regime should be replaced by a more moderate and democratic government.

Trujillo's rule had created widespread dissatisfaction in the Dominican Republic and there were numerous dissidents who desired his overthrow. Early in 1960, the CIA began to develop contacts with dissident leaders. On July 1, a CIA memo that recommended the delivery of sniper rifles to the dissidents was approved and the following January, the shipment of a "limited supply of small arms and other material" was likewise granted approval.

Between February 10 and 15, 1961, meetings were held in New York between CIA officials and dissident leaders from the Dominican Republic. The Dominicans requested further aid in the form of carbines, pistols, and other weapons. They also described a plan of action to bring down Trujillo that included a rebel force of 300 men, armed with the requested weapons, explosive devices, and remote control detonation devices. In the following two months, the CIA approved many of the dissidents' requests.

But then came mid-April, 1961, and the failure of the Bay of Pigs invasion. The embarrassment felt by the Kennedy administration was acute. Fearful of further CIA operations—and failures—in the Caribbean, the Agency began quickly to withdraw from its commitments and promises to the Dominican dissidents. Arms shipments were halted and new requests from the dissidents were denied.

The dissidents, however, continued with their plans. President Kennedy, warned that the overthrow and probable assassination of Trujillo was imminent, advised a State

Department representative in the Dominican Republic on May 29 that the United States "must not run risk of U.S. association with political assassination." This principle, the president advised, is "overriding" and "must prevail in doubtful situations."

Kennedy's note, however, added that if the dissidents overthrew Trujillo and were successful in establishing a new government, the United States would recognize them. The following day, May 30, President Trujillo was ambushed and murdered near the Dominican city of San Cristobal. The Church Committee concluded that there was no direct involvement by the Agency in the assassination, but that the CIA had done much to encourage the climate that led to Trujillo's death.

The Case of Ngo Dinh Diem. Diem's overthrow and assassination were discussed in Chapter Seven. As in the case of Trujillo, the Church Committee found no direct CIA involvement, but concluded that the Agency had helped create the climate that led to the coup d'état and to Diem's death.

The Case of General René Schneider. In 1970, General Schneider was chief of staff of Chile's armed forces. A moderate man, he cherished his country's democratic traditions and honored the separation of military from political life. It was Schneider's duty to remain aloof from politics and oversee his country's security.

However, 1970 was a year of crisis in Chile which saw the election of a Marxist, Salvador Allende, as president. Allende's election aroused deep anxiety among conservatives in Chile and policy makers in Washington, who believed that an Allende government would pave the way for communism in Chile. Allende made no secret of his admiration for Fidel Castro and Castro's revolution in Cuba.

On September 15, 1970, President Nixon instructed CIA Director Richard Helms to see that the Agency did everything in its power to prevent Allende from assuming the presidency. By early October, the CIA was in contact with conservative dissident members of Chile's military establishment. The dissidents included retired General Roberto Viaux and General Valenzuela. From General Viaux, CIA operatives learned that the dissidents planned to carry out a program of action against Allende, the first stage of which would be the kidnapping of General Schneider. Schneider's kidnapping, the dissidents believed, would create a crisis in Chile which could be exploited by the conservatives to undermine Allende.

On October 15, the CIA informed National Security Advisor Henry Kissinger and the White House of the Viaux plot. Despite its fears of an Allende presidency, the White House reacted to news of the plot negatively. Viaux's plans sounded too vague and dangerous, and the CIA was ordered to defuse the plot, at least temporarily. Two days later, agents in Chile informed Viaux of the White House reaction, but the retired general replied that the plans would proceed in any event and the first step would remain the kidnapping of Schneider.

On October 19, a first attempt was made to kidnap Schneider, and failed. On October 20, a second attempt likewise ended in failure. But on the morning of October 22, two days before the Chilean legislature was to confirm Allende's election by secret ballot, General Schneider was stopped while driving from his home to his office. Four young men surrounded him and when he resisted their efforts to kidnap him, they shot him in the neck and stomach. The general died three days later, the first prominent Chilean leader to be the victim of assassination in 140 years.

The Church committee reported that there was no evidence to link the CIA with the assassination. It did, however, conclude that the urgency for Allende's removal that the White House had expressed, created an atmosphere that contributed to the general's death. The CIA may not have planned the assassination, but it knew of the plans to kidnap Schneider and made no warning to the proper authorities.

The committee also noted that requests from the dissidents for weapons had been approved by the CIA and that these weapons had been delivered to Chile in the week prior to the assassination. The CIA weapons had not been used in the assassination, but such actions, the committee implied, hardly showed CIA disapproval for the course of action planned by the rebels.

Who Was to Blame?

The Church committee report pointed out that four of the five plots against foreign leaders occurred between 1960 and 1965, during "the depths of the Cold War," and at a time when the Soviet-American rivalry had become very bitter. This atmosphere helped to explain the plots, the report said, but it could never "justify" them. Nevertheless, it was clear that those involved believed that they were doing the best thing for their country in the worldwide struggle against communism.

The plots could not be justified, the report continued, for three reasons. First, none of the plots were "necessitated by imminent danger to the United States." The one exception was Castro. Yet, he was a threat to American security only during the Cuban Missile Crisis of October, 1962, while plots against his life had been carried out before the crisis and were continued afterward. In the case of Lumumba, the only other plot in which the committee found evidence of direct CIA involvement, there was no imminent threat to the United States.

Second, the committee believed that the United States could not justify its actions by the standards of totalitarian nations. "Our standards must be higher," the committee maintained, "and this difference is what the struggle is all about."

This country was created by violent revolt against a regime believed to be tyrannous, and our founding fathers (the local dissidents of that era) received aid from foreign countries. Given that history, we should not today rule out support for dissident groups seeking to overthrow tyrants.

But any support granted by the United States, the report went on, should raise serious questions: what tactics should be used? should the aid be overt or covert? and how should the actions be authorized by our government? None of these questions had been seriously considered by the CIA.

The third reason the committee believed the assassination plots unjustified was that "such activities almost inevitably become known." They do not remain secret, nor can they be plausibly denied. They become public and reflect on the reputation of the United States abroad and undermine the confidence the American people have in their government at home.

The vagueness surrounding the origins of the plots especially troubled the Church committee. No direct orders from a president could be found in any of the cases which showed that the chief executive had expressly ordered the assassination plot initiated. There were only general instructions, such as "somthing will have to be done about Castro" and "Trujillo will have to go."

But it was clear, the committee said, that CIA officials believed that the plots had been fully authorized from above and that they were carrying out the wishes of the president. "This failure of communication," the report concluded, "was inexcusable in light of the gravity of assassination." In the future, the CIA's way of conducting business would have to be changed so that directives from the president to the CIA were clear and distinct.

The committee noted that in 1972, CIA Director Richard Helms had issued the first directive against assassination and that in 1973, a similar directive had been issued by his successor, William Colby. The Helms directive had read:

It has recently again been alleged in the press that CIA engages in assassination. As you are well aware, this is not the case, and Agency policy has long been clear on the issue. To underline it, however, I direct that no such activity or operation be undertaken, assisted or suggested by any of our personnel.

The Colby directive was more succinct:

CIA will not engage in assassination nor induce, assist or suggest to others that assassination be employed.

And at a press conference on June 9, 1975, President Ford declared that he too was opposed to assassination. "This administration," Ford said, "has not and will not use such means as instruments of national policy."

In its recommendations for CIA reform, the Church committee welcomed these statements, but believed that more

[130]

was needed. "Administrations change, CIA directors change," the report pointed out, "and someday in the future what was tried in the past may once again become a temptation."

> *Assassination plots did happen. It would be irresponsible not to do all that can be done to prevent their happening again. A law is needed. Laws express our nation's values; they deter those who might be tempted to ignore those values and stiffen the will of those who want to resist the temptation.*

The law suggested by the committee would make it a criminal offense for persons subject to the jurisdiction of the United States (1) to conspire, within or outside America to assassinate a foreign official, (2) to attempt to assassinate a foreign official, or (3) to assassinate a foreign official. Such a law, the committee believed, would be the best way to eliminate assassination plots in the future.

The Question of Chile

CIA activity in Chile was not unique. It was similar to operations the Agency had carried out in Italy beginning in 1948 and to the operations in Iran and elsewhere. Nor was the Chilean operation the largest CIA program—that distinction had to go to the Agency's activities in Southeast Asia.

What made the CIA's work in Chile of particular interest to the Senate committee was the tragic outcome of that work. In 1973, Chilean President Salvador Allende died during a coup d'état directed against his regime by conservative generals. Furthermore, Allende, who had been legally elected by the people of Chile, was replaced by a military dictatorship that brought an end to the long tradition of democracy in Chile. Had the CIA played a part in these events?

Rumors of CIA involvement in Chilean political life had been widespread for several years before the Church committee began its investigation. On February 7, 1973, at Senate hearings on the confirmation of Richard Helms to be ambassador to Iran, the former director of central intelligence was asked about these rumors. His questioner was Senator Stuart Symington (Democrat, Missouri):

[131]

SENATOR SYMINGTON. Did you try in the Central Intelligence Agency to overthrow the Government of Chile?
MR. HELMS. No, sir.

SENATOR SYMINGTON. Did you have any money passed to the opponents of Allende?
MR. HELMS. No, sir.

SENATOR SYMINGTON. So the stories you were involved in that war are wrong?
MR. HELMS. Yes, sir. I said to Senator Fulbright many months ago that if the Agency had really gotten in behind the other candidates and spent a lot of money and so forth the election might have come out differently.

Two years later, the Church investigation was to show that Helms lied in response to the questions put to him by Senator Symington. CIA activity in Chile had been pervasive, and its financial support to Allende's opponents had been abundant. Helms, who had had a distinguished career in the Agency, had lied to protect CIA secrets which he believed should not be made public. But his misrepresentations were later to cause him acute embarrassment and add to the controversy that surrounded the CIA operation in Chile.

Contrary to Helms's testimony, the Church committee found that the CIA had spent large sums of money in Chile. For the years from 1963 through 1973, and rounded to the nearest $100,000, these sums broke down as follows:

Propaganda for Elections and
Other Support for Political Parties $8,000,000

Producing and Disseminating
Propaganda and Supporting Mass Media $4,300,000

Influencing Chilean Institutions:
(labor, students, peasants, women) and
Supporting Private Sector Organizations $900,000

Promoting Military Coup d'État   Less than $200,000

These figures add up to more than $13 million.

Why had this money been spent? During the early years of CIA involvement in Chilean politics, the money had been spent to create a strong moderate political force and to strengthen parties that would resist the extremism of both the left and right. In 1970 and afterward, however, expenditures were directed toward the defeat of Allende.

How was the money spent? It was spent in a variety of ways, ranging from the production of political leaflets to the supply of weapons to dissidents. American involvement in Chile began in 1962, when the CIA gave $230,000 to the Christian Democratic Party and its leader Eduardo Frei. The Christian Democrats were regarded as Chile's strongest moderate party and the one most likely to draw votes away from the left.

In 1964—a presidential election year in Chile—the Agency added $3 million to its gifts to the Christian Democrats and then approved a supplement of $160,000 which was earmarked for support of Christian Democrat slum dwellers' and peasants' organizations. The gifts paid off. On September 4, Frei, a moderate leftist, was elected president with 55.7 percent of the vote. During his six years in office, Frei pursued a policy of moderate reforms designed to improve the lot of Chile's urban and rural poor. At the same time, the CIA continued its financial support of moderate parties and their candidates.

As 1970, the next presidential election year approached, however, there was growing concern in Washington and among Chile's conservatives. Under Chile's constitution, Frei could not succeed himself and there was no moderate candidate of comparable stature and popularity to replace him. A union of leftist parties under Salvador Allende called the Popular Unity (UP) appeared to be gaining strength.

As early as April 15, 1969, the question of Chile's presidential election was raised at a meeting of President Nixon's intelligence advisers. A CIA representative at the meeting warned that action would have to come soon, if the outcome of the election, now seventeen months away, was to be affected. On March 25, 1970, $125,000 was approved for "a spoiling operation against Allende's party" and in the following months considerable additional sums were likewise approved.

The CIA funding of the Allende opposition, however,

[133]

proved to be insufficient. On September 4, Allende won 36.3 percent of the vote—a margin of 39,000 votes out of 3,000,000 votes cast in the election. His nearest opponent, Jorge Alessandri, received 35.3 percent. The election then went to the Chilean legislature, which would choose between the two candidates with the highest number of votes.

Allende's victory sent a wave of concern through Washington. On September 15, President Nixon ordered Richard Helms, the CIA Director, to prevent Allende's accession to office. Helms then initiated what came to be known as Track II, a program of direct CIA involvement in Chile that concentrated on the removal of Allende. On September 16, at an off-the-record White House press briefing, National Security Advisor Henry Kissinger stated the administration's belief that Allende's election had created "massive problems" for the U.S. and Latin America.

In late October, the Chilean legislature approved of Allende over Alessandri by a vote of 153 to 35 and on November 3, the new president was formally sworn into office. The character of Allende's program for Chile soon emerged. In December, he proposed a constitutional amendment that would establish state control of the country's large mines. And in July of the following year, the amendment was passed unanimously at a joint session of the legislature.

The amendment provided for the nationalization of the copper industry, which was primarily American-owned. Compensation was to be provided to the copper companies, but, Allende warned, "excess profits" made by the companies would be deducted from the compensation. On September 29, the Chilean government took control of the Chilean Telephone Company (CHITELCO), 70 percent of which had been owned by the American corporation ITT since 1930.

By the time the copper industry had been nationalized, however, the CIA was already deeply involved in its program of political and economic sabotage. Between 1970 and 1973, the Agency spent $8 million in its drive to unseat Allende—$3 million were spent in 1972 alone. A large portion of the money went to influence the media and carry out a program of anti-Allende propaganda. Newspapers and radio stations were purchased and $700,000 went to support the prominent Santiago daily, *El Mercurio.*

Subsidies were continued and stepped up to the Christian Democrats and to other moderate parties. At the same time, efforts were made to split the UP, Allende's coalition of the left. CIA money was likewise spent on candidates in municipal and legislative elections whom the Agency regarded as friendly to American interests.

At least one large American corporation, ITT, became involved in the attempt to bring down the Allende government. As early as June, 1970, discussions had taken place between John McCone, a director of ITT and former CIA director, and Richard Helms, the current CIA director. In July and September, Harold Geneen, the president of ITT, offered huge sums of money—in one case as much as $1 million—to help the CIA stop Allende.

The Agency refused the ITT aid, but at least $50,000 of ITT funds found their way into the treasury of Allende's opponent, Jorge Alessandri. In October, 1971, ITT presented the White House with an eighteen-point plan to see that Allende "does not get through the crucial next six months." The plan included a series of economic and political measures to be taken against the Allende government. It was rejected by the president and his advisers, however, because they preferred to handle the problem in their own way.

It is difficult to determine the extent to which the CIA contributed to Allende's downfall, because Allende's own political and economic bungling played its part. Elected with little more than one-third of the vote, Allende acted as though he had a much larger mandate. His economic programs earned him the dislike of many Chileans, and his steady move to the left, especially when Fidel Castro was an honored guest in Chile in 1971, aroused the suspicions of moderates.

Strikes and other forms of discontent became commonplace. Late in 1971, the Christian Democrats and the National Party organized the "March of the Empty Pots," a march by housewives to protest food shortages. In 1972, there were strikes by the shopkeepers of Santiago and by the Confederation of Truck Owners. In 1973, miners, physicians, teachers, students, bus and taxi drivers, and the Confederation of Professional Employees went out on strike at various times in the late spring and early summer. Despite numerous allegations to the contrary, the CIA did not encourage these strikes.

By the summer of 1973, the political crisis had become acute. 100,000 Allende supporters marched in celebration of the president's election to office three years earlier, but this show of approval was too little and too late. On September 11, the conspirators carried out a coup d'état against the Marxist president. Allende died in the confusion of the coup, a reported suicide.

The Church committee asked three direct questions about the role played by the CIA in the fall of Allende:

• "Was the United States directly involved, covertly, in the 1973 events in Chile?" The committee found no evidence of direct U.S. involvement in the coup that overthrew Allende and resulted in his death. But it did note that continued U.S. support for the overthrow of the government offered encouragement to the dissidents.

• "Did the U.S. provide covert support to striking truck owners or other strikes during 1971–1973." Here again there was no evidence of direct CIA support for the strikes. It was clear, however, that the Agency had given support to groups that backed the strikes.

• "Did the U.S. provide covert support to right-wing terrorist organizations during 1970-1973?" The Committee found that CIA help had been given to one organization "whose tactics became more violent over time."

A December 7, 1975, editorial in *The New York Times* succinctly summarized the findings of the Select Committee on Intelligence . "The staff report," the editorial said, ". . . has now placed the activities of the United States Government in Chile in some perspective."

The central fact that emerges is that although the United States did inexcusably interfere in the Chilean political process, the United States still was not basically respon-

sible for the overthrow of President Salvador Allende. Despite the left-wing myth that this country was the prime mover in that event, the coup was actually conceived and carried out by Chileans acting for reasons of their own.

By the end of 1973, the military junta that now governed Chile had declared Marxist parties illegal and had placed all other parties in indefinite recess. Press censorship was established and the arrests—and in some cases summary executions—of thousands of political "undesirables" were reported. On June 20, 1975, General Pinochet, the head of the military junta, declared that there "will be no elections in Chile during my lifetime nor in the lifetime of my successor."

At the conclusion of its report on Chile, the Church committee recommended that in the future, covert action "should be resorted to only to counter severe threats to the national security of the United States." It is far from clear, the report went on, "that this was the case in Chile."

The committee claimed to offer no final judgment "on the political propriety, the morality, or even the effectiveness of American covert activity in Chile." But it did point out that the United States, by its covert actions, was seen "to have contradicted not only its official declarations but its treaty commitments and principles of long standing."

There are many long-term effects of covert actions.... The Chilean institutions that the United States most favored may have been discredited.... In Latin America particularly, even the suspicion of CIA support may be the kiss of death. It would be the final irony of the decade of covert action in Chile if that action destroyed the credibility of the Chilean Christian Democrats.

The recommendations of the Church committee in the matter of the assassination plots and covert action in Chile were an attempt to bring the CIA under the rule of law. They reflected the concerns of a Senate that had passed through the Vietnam War and the Watergate Affair—both cases where many observers believed that government had overstepped its authority and violated the American Constitution and American traditions. The ideals represented in the Church committee report—openness in policy making and caution in the exercise of power—were ideals most people could support, but only up to a point. In the years that followed the publication of the committee's report, the United States began to grow more conservative. And with this new conservatism appeared the belief that certain ideals had to be sacrificed for the sake of national security. These ideals need not be forgotten, the conservatives would argue, but realism and wisdom insist that they be balanced with concerns for the protection of American interests.

CHAPTER TEN

EPILOGUE

*"The difficulties of the past decade
are behind us."*

**A 1981 statement
by the new CIA director,
William J. Casey**

The CIA controversy of the 1970s produced surprisingly little legislation to restrain the activities of the Agency. In 1974, the Congress passed a significant amendment to the Foreign Assistance Act. The amendment provided that before the Agency could spend funds on covert action, it had to receive presidential approval and submit a "timely report" to Congress. As Senator Harold Hughes (Democrat, Iowa), one of the bill's sponsors, stated in its defense:

the amendment I offer should be regarded as only a beginning toward the imperative of imposing some order and structure to the means by which the American people, through their elected representatives, can exercise a measure of control over the cloak-and-dagger operations of the intelligence agencies of the U.S. government.

Senator Hughes's amendment turned out to be one of the few meaningful pieces of CIA-related legislation passed by Congress in the 1970s. The principal reason for this was the assassination of the CIA's station chief in Athens, Greece, Richard S. Welch, on December 23, 1975, by a terrorist squad.

Welch's identify as a CIA agent had first been revealed in *CounterSpy,* a Washington, D.C., magazine with connections to Philip Agee, the ex-CIA agent turned bitter critic of the Agency. Welch's murder awakened new concern among the American people about the safety and security of the members of the intelligence community. Had criticism of the CIA been carried too far? Were the investigations of the Agency endangering the quality of American intelligence? These concerns were reflected in Congress.

As a result, much of the impetus for CIA reform passed from the House and Senate of the president. President Ford responded with Executive Order 11905 on February 18, 1976. Ford's order provided for some reorganization of the Agency and established the Committee on Foreign Intelligence, which was to have power to oversee CIA budgeting and policy problems. But Ford's order had little real effect on the questions raised by critics during the height of the CIA controversy.

President Jimmy Carter exercised other, more meaningful changes. The most important of these was an act signed by Carter which provided for a depth of congressional review over intelligence operations that surpasses anything previously granted to the legislature of a democratic country. Known as the Intelligence Oversight Act, it gives House and Senate intelligence committees the right to be kept currently informed on all intelligence activities to which they demand access.

Under the administration of conservative Republican Ronald Reagan, however, attitudes toward the CIA have changed. The new administration gives every indication that it plans to strengthen the Agency and to allow it more secrecy in its operations. Reagan's CIA director, William J. Casey, who was a member of the OSS during World War II, has said that "our emphasis from now on should be to maintain and enhance CIA's reputation . . . by the excellence of our work and the high quality of our contribution."

Casey has halted the occasional background briefings provided reporters since the days of Allen Dulles. Issuance of public reports and studies by the CIA will likewise probably be discontinued. The new Agency leadership firmly believes that the CIA should not be called upon to play a public role.

The primary reason for the strengthening of the CIA and the return to what many observers believe will be the Agency of the past is concern over the Soviet Union. During the 1970s, according to many experts, the Soviet Union rapidly improved its armed forces until its military might is now greater than that of the United States. And the USSR gave evidence of that military might—and of Soviet aggressiveness—by its invasion of Afghanistan in 1979. The Reagan administration believes that the Soviet Union is "on the move" throughout the world and that the present world situation calls for renewed American military power and renewed assertion of American interests and needs.

The role played by the CIA in the 1980s will probably be significant. President Reagan has expressed concern about several trouble spots, the chief of which are the Central American nation of El Salvador and the African nation of Angola. In El Salvador, leftist guerrillas are fighting to unseat an American-supported government; in Angola, an anti-communist guerrilla force is struggling to overcome the Marxist regime. In the future, CIA activity may be expanded in areas such as these.

The Reagan administration has also listed terrorism as a number one priority, and no agency in the federal government is better prepared or designed to deal with terrorism than the CIA. In the summer of 1981, the Agency issued a report on terrorism that traced support for terrorist bands to the Soviet Union and the Soviet Union's allies, Libya and Cuba. The report, too, pointed to the alarming rate of increase in terrorism in recent years and to the fact that the targets of terrorist acts are frequently American businessmen and others representing the United States abroad.

In July, 1981, a new scandal struck the Agency. Max Hugel, the deputy director of operations (the section in charge of clandestine affairs) and an appointee of CIA Director Casey, was accused by former business associates of gross financial improprieties and dishonesty. Hugel vehemently denied the allegations but nevertheless resigned his post. It seemed a bad beginning for an Agency now on the comeback after years of embroilment in controversy.

[142]

The Hugel affair reflected badly on Director Casey, who had warmly supported his appointment. And Casey's reputation also fell under a shadow. The new CIA director was accused of misrepresenting past financial dealings in testimony he gave before the Senate Intelligence Committee during his confirmation hearings. He was likewise said to have withheld information from the committee about his present financial status.

For several days, it seemed that Casey, like Hugel, would be forced to resign. But with the firm support of President Reagan, Casey weathered the storm. The new director was allowed to stay at his post and the Senate Intelligence Committee withdrew its criticisms, "pending further investigation."

The new, conservative Congress had little interest in further challenging or undermining the reputation of the CIA. Gone were the days of the 1970s when the Congress and the American public clamored for investigations of alleged wrongdoing. The most important CIA-related legislation before the new Congress of the 1980s was a bill that sought to protect the names of CIA agents from publication—and thereby protect them from the fate that befell Richard Welch in Athens.

From its beginning in 1947 until the present day, the CIA has reflected the needs and concerns of the American people and government. During the height of the cold war, it functioned as a secret organization combating the spread of communism. During the political changes and upheavals of the 1960s and 1970s, it was affected by the public demand for openness and accountability of government. And now, as cold war fears once again are on the rise, the CIA is seeking to return to the image it fostered in the 1950s, hoping, in the words of the director, "that the difficulties of the past decade are behind."

ADDITIONAL READING

The number of books, magazine articles, and other sources of material on the CIA is very large. The works listed here are the ones this author has found most useful and informative. Books of special interest to younger readers are marked with an asterisk (*).

The Government Investigations:

U.S. Congress. Senate Select Committee to Study Governmental Operations with Respect to Intelligence Activities. *Foreign and Military Intelligence,* Book I, and *Intelligence Activities and the Rights of Americans,* Book II. 94th Congress, 2nd Session, April 26, 1976. Report number 94-755. This is the Church committee report.*

_____. *Alleged Assassination Plots Involving Foreign Leaders: Interim Report.* 94th Congress, 1st session, 20 November 1975.*

_____. *Covert Action in Chile 1963-1973: Staff Report.* 94th Congress, 1st session, 1975.*

Report to the President by the Commission on CIA Activities Within the United States. Washington, DC: Government

Printing Office, June, 1975. This is the Rockefeller Commission report.*

Buncher, Judith, editor. *The CIA & the Security Debate: 1971-1975.* New York: Facts on File, 1976. An excellent collection of documents relating to the CIA controversy.*

Fain, Tyrus G., *et al.,* editors. *The Intelligence Community: History, Organization, and Issues.* Public Documents Series. New York: R.R. Bowker Company, 1977. An excellent digest of government documents and reports relating to the CIA.*

The History of the CIA:

Corson, William. *The Armies of Ignorance: The Rise of the American Intelligence Empire.* New York: The Dial Press/ James Wade, 1977.

Jeffreys-Jones, Rhodri. *American Espionage from Secret Service to CIA.* New York: The Free Press, 1977.*

Kirkpatrick, Lyman. *The Real CIA.* New York: Macmillan, 1968.*

Ransom, Harry Howe. *The Intelligence Establishment.* Cambridge: Harvard University Press, 1970.

Tully, Andrew. *CIA: The Inside Story.* New York: William Morrow and Company, 1962. Very readable.*

CIA Autobiographies and Biographies:

Colby, William, and Peter Forbath. *Honorable Men: My Life in the CIA.* New York: Simon & Schuster, 1978.*

Dulles, Allen Welsh. *The Craft of Intelligence.* New York: Harper & Row, 1963.*

Phillips, David Atlee. *The Night Watch.* New York: Atheneum, 1977. Phillips was a CIA specialist in Latin America.*

Powers, Thomas. *The Man Who Kept the Secrets: Richard Helms & the CIA.* New York: Knopf, 1979. Very informative.*

de Silva, Peer. *Sub Rosa: The CIA and the Use of Intelligence.* New York: Times Books, 1978.*

Smith, Joseph Burkholder. *Portrait of a Cold Warrior.* New York: G.P. Putnam's Sons, 1976.*

CIA: Methods and Techniques:

Cline, Ray S. *Secrets, Spies and Scholars: Blueprint of the Essential CIA.* Washington, D.C.: Acropolis Books, 1976.

Copeland, Miles. *The Game of Nations.* New York: Simon & Schuster, 1969.

————. *Without Cloak or Dagger: The Truth About the New Espionage.* New York: Simon & Schuster, 1974.

The Critics of the CIA:

Agee, Philip. *Inside the Company: CIA Diary.* New York: Stonehill, 1975.

Gravel, Michael, editor. *The Senator Mike Gravel Edition— The Pentagon Papers.* Boston: The Beacon Press, 1971.

Langguth, A.J. *Hidden Terrors.* New York: Pantheon Books, 1978.

McGarvey, Patrick J. *CIA: The Myth and the Madness.* New York: Saturday Review Press, 1972.*

Marchetti, Victor and John D. Marks. *The CIA and the Cult of Intelligence.* New York: Knopf, 1974.*

Marks, John. *The Search for the "Manchurian Candidate": The CIA and Mind Control.* New York: Times Books, 1979.*

Wise, David, and Thomas Ross. *The Invisible Government.* New York: Random House, 1964.*

INDEX